We Are Theologians

Strengthening the People of the Episcopal Church

Fredrica Harris Thompsett

1 9 8 9

Cowley Publications

Cambridge, Massachusetts

International Standard Book Number: 0-936384-68-9
Library of Congress Number: 88-39445

Cover Design by Daniel Earl Thaxton

Library of Congress Cataloging-in-Publications Data
Thompsett, Fredrica Harris, 1942–
    We are theologians : strengthening the people of the
    Episcopal Church/ Fredrica Harris Thompsett.
       p. cm.
    Bibliography: p.
    Includes index.
    ISBN 0-936384-68-9 : $8.95
    1. Identification (Religion) 2.. Episcopal Church—
Doctrines. 3. Anglican Communion—Doctrines. 4. Liberation theology. 5. Christianity—20th century. I. Title.
BV4509.5.T485 1989
248.4'83—dc19   88-39445

Cowley Publications
980 Memorial Drive
Cambridge, MA 02138

Second Printing

DEDICATION

For
Bruce Alfred Thompsett
(1939-1987)
"Love is as strong as death."
(Song of Solomon 8: 6)

PRAISE FOR
We Are Theologians

"This is the most thoughtful, clear and stimulating book on the ministry of the laity that I have read since reading *The Theology of the Laity* by Hendrik Kraemer a generation ago. . . . It is Anglican Theology at its best and precisely relevant for the last decade of the twentieth century for the mission of the church."

—John Coburn
from the Preface

"Thompsett uses a wide-angle lens to give us a revitalized understanding of the church. She summons us all to the adventure of change."

—Marianne H. Micks

"Invites her readers to embark upon a search for definition and meaning in Holy Scriptures, in the history and theology of the church and in contemporary life."

—Mary Sudman Donovan

"Parish educators take note: . . .old and new members alike will have a clearer picture of how we all must take responsibility for our future as the church."

—Prof. Flower Ross
Seabury-Western Theol. Seminary

ACKNOWLEDGEMENTS

This book began in earnest with hospitable invitations from friends, old and new. I am indebted to members of the Province III Conference of the Episcopal Church—informally and generally known as the "Hood Conference"—who in the summer of 1984 welcomed and listened to keynote lectures which became the first draft of this volume. At other public conferences along the way I gathered courage and labored to speak directly with and among communities of adult learners. Laity and clergy in the Episcopal Dioceses of Florida, Ohio, Arkansas, Central New York, and Eastern Oregon have provided focused occasions for teaching and learning. I have been challenged and sustained by participation in several Province I Continuing Education Convocations.

Faculty and student colleagues of three seminaries where I have been fortunate to profess my love of church history and, most particularly, the community of the Episcopal Divinity School, have offered truthfulness conveyed in diversity.

A 1987-88 grant from the Conant Fund, administered by the Episcopal Church's Board for Theological Education, as well as the support of both faculty and administration, sustained my first full sabbatical in twenty years of teaching. Three students, now alumnae and alumni of the Episcopal Divinity School—Linda Naef, Richard Godbolt and Elisabeth Gomes—served well as research assistants and inquiring critics.

Most of all Dorothy Brittain, long-time friend and theological wise woman, heard me into speech, offering courage and hospitality along the way.

Among these and other mutual friends I continue to discover that the voice of the church is the voice of the people, or as early Tudor reformers would have noted, *Vox Populi, Vox Dei.*

Fredrica Harris Thompsett
Cambridge, Massachusetts

PREFACE
by John Coburn

This is the most thoughtful, clear and stimulating book on the ministry of the laity that I have read since reading *The Theology of the Laity* by Hendrik Kraemer a generation ago. Like his book, this one by Fredrica Harris Thompsett will, I believe, be recognized as a "a minor classic" which explains realistically and hopefully the role of laity in carrying forward the mission of the church in contemporary society.

If clergy take this analysis to heart and together with laity put it into practice in their parishes, there is promised a renewal of the church, a better biblically educated membership, a deepened spirit of evangelism and a stronger commitment to the Gospel and its mission. It encourages clergy to set lay persons free to be "the Church in the world" that they are meant to be.

Since many clergy prefer to control laity rather than set them free perhaps bishops should give copies of this book to all their clergy—having first "read, marked and inwardly digested" its contents themselves.

In any case, here is an analysis of our Anglican (but not too Anglican) tradition with its emphasis upon engagement with both the biblical revelation and the issues of contemporary society. Ms. Thompsett puts into clear historical perspective the distinctive insights of the Reformation, the particular contribution of lay persons to the mission of the Church in the nineteenth century in America and concludes with the most balanced, intelligible discussion of the significance of contemporary liberation theology with which I am familiar.

Ms. Thompsett re-examines our tradition, brings it up-to-date, and encourages us to press forward with confidence and hope into a future which, however unclear, is always—for Christians—promising.

This book is both "comforting"—i.e. "strengthening"—and challenging. It is hopeful, not strident, written in a graceful style easy to read and to understand. It is Anglican theology at its best and precisely relevant for the last decade of the twentieth century for the mission of the Church.

John B. Coburn
Boston, Massachusetts

Table of Contents

GOD'S WORK—AND OURS 1
A Voyage of Discovery   1
Standing the Bible on Its Feet   5
Book of Books, Our People's Strength   12
Inviting Ourselves into God's Story   19

LOOKING BACKWARD, THINKING FORWARD . 27
Remembering the People   27
People of the Book   32
"I Must Be Up and Doing!"   40
"The Real Battles of the Faith"   50

ALL CAN BE THEOLOGIANS 57
Knowing Who We Are   57
"All Can Be Theologians"   64
Digesting Biblical Knowledge   68
Rejoicing in Creation   75
Changing Lives   79

SEEKING WIDER LOYALTIES: Today's Theologies of Liberation 87
Hearing and Knowing   87
Social and Personal Transformation   94
Voicing Local Theologies   101

IDEAS TO GROW ON 115
Making Room for the Future   115
Renewing Perspectives   122
Seeking Hospitality   128

SELECTED FOR FURTHER READING 141

INDEX 147

GOD'S WORK—AND OURS

A Voyage of Discovery

There is an excitement to exploration, a rush of adrenaline that comes from starting out on a journey, an energy that comes from discovering that we are on the right path, and an expectation that despite the risks we shall return wiser than we left. Yet humility is essential. Knowledge often turns us toward our roots, our earliest understandings. This is especially true for Christians. Our voyages of discovery have a way of sending us homeward, raising basic questions about our inheritance, our identity, our purpose. These lines from T. S. Eliot's *Four Quartets* set a clear direction for those in search of understanding:

> We shall not cease from exploration
> And the end of all our exploring
> Will be to arrive where we started
> And know the place for the first time.

With our hearts and minds open to receive surprises, new learnings, old truths, timeless meanings, Christian pilgrims are not so much inventors but explorers, discoverers of what has been there all along.

This is a hopeful way to begin asking the question, "What does it mean to be Christians today?" The question is a complex one, but our responses need not be complicated. The sources for exploring Christian identity are familiar ones that have guided faithful people throughout the ages: the Bible, various cultural histories, and theological inheritances. Still, questions proliferate when we set out to discover our mission. What is our mission as members of a local congregation, as participants in a Christian denomination, as part of Christianity worldwide? What do we believe is the nature and purpose of the church? What is our theology, our doctrine about membership in a church? What images of the church inspire us, and what images oppress us? What have laity to do with shaping the work of the church? What hopes do we have for the mission, the ethical character, of the church in a new decade, indeed, of all Christians in a new millennium?

These are all questions about "ecclesiology," the formal theological term for understanding the church. They are also questions about the fundamental nature of Christian life, foundational questions for all baptized persons. Whether implicit or explicit, our theology of the church, our ecclesiology, shapes expectations for the church's work in the world.

This is particularly true for laity. In this technological society, ordained ministers and other religious professionals are usually defined functionally. Such definitions may not be adequate, but in an increasingly secular society we are in danger of identifying what the church is with what the ordained do! I am not at all worried about clarifying the role and purpose of ordination; there is a seemingly endless bibliography on this subject dating from the second century, and clergy today continue to address this question. Yet I am worried that the church will become a clerical reservation, a preserve that can only be fully understood and embodied by clergy. If we wish to embrace the image and reality of an engaged, expansive church, then our theology of the church both depends upon, and must be convincing to, lay people. Despite rhetorical flourishes about valuing and enabling "lay ministry" (a redundant and awkward phrase), practical, effective definitions of the church as all the people of God, 99% of whom are laity, are beginning to disappear.

Laity have already disappeared from much conventional theology, ecclesiastical history, and even popular biblical imagery. In his pioneering book, *The Theology of the Laity*, Hendrik Kraemer pointed to the "amazing fact" that the laity have not been *"theologically* relevant in the Church's thinking about itself." Kraemer insists that the critical significance of the laity demands a new, whole ecclesiology. Entire histories of the church have been written that dwell on scenes of clerical life as if laity were not a crucial contributors and leaders. More recently historians have begun to pay attention to the common folk, to what has been described as "popular religion." Critical scholars are rejecting the implicit two-tiered "producer/consumer" model of supposedly articulate clergy developing doctrine for presumably inarticulate laity. Yet even well-intentioned modern authors have suggested that lay initiatives were usually suppressed by the institutional church and thus laity were not makers and shakers of religious life. Those who seek to liberate laity by telling only the "bad news" of how laity have been oppressed and by denying the record of lay achievements err doubly. One of the themes of this book that will recur over and over is that memory is essential to liberation. Generations of Christians cannot be counted as sheep. Common sense and historical data suggest otherwise. Many devotional books also promote erroneous interpretations by emphasizing individual saints, rather than the central story of God's covenant with the people. One precocious preacher's child explained to me that the halos over the heads of Peter and

3

Paul meant they were ordained. Our images of the church as the whole people of God biblically, historically and theologically, as well as practically and ethically, are in need of revision, renewal, and expansion. We have settled for a church that is too small.

In her recent book, *The Authority of the Laity*, Verna Dozier depicts the church as a "sleeping giant," a large corporate body that only needs to awaken to its full potential, its God-given mission. If we wish to awaken the sleeping giant, the people of God, the Bible has for centuries been the place to start. It yields basic, abundant testimony for a whole ecclesiology. It reveals images and tells stories of God's chosen people as they journey in the wilderness. It prompts us to "remember the past" accurately. Of course we know this. We've heard many, if not most, of the biblical stories before. As one little girl wrote in a letter addressed to God, "Could you write more stories? We have already read all the ones you have and begin again."

Perhaps, to quote T. S. Eliot, "We had the experience but missed the meaning."

If our vision of the church is meager or even modest, we have missed the mighty acts of God. If we think of Christians as hopelessly embattled, we have lost our ancestors' experience of the expansion of God's reign. If we reject biblical wisdom because we see the Bible used as a tool for legalistic oppression, we have forgotten the Gospel's response to Pharisees, the way in which Jesus's liberating ministry threatened the religious establishment of his own day. If we think religious complacency and indifference are modern habits, we have overlooked the complaints of the biblical prophets. And if we think the question, "What does the Bible have to do with my life?" sheds more light on heaven than on our work on earth, we have lost the creative essence of God's work.

This book concentrates on the work of the laity in biblical, historical, theological, contemporary and future perspectives. This viewpoint is not intended to exclude clergy, they are obviously members of the great *laos tou theou*, the Greek phrase for the chosen people of God. Stories of clerical life will continue to be told in other volumes. My panorama is larger, more akin to the biblical landscape. I prefer to review images and episodes in the lives of God's ordinary people. I want to pursue insights that contribute to a whole ecclesiology. I aim to create snapshots, "re-visions" of basic Christian stories, whose meanings are accessible to clergy and laity. My quest is for familiar and contemporary resources, my desire is to seek out and explore what it means to be members of the Christian church in the closing decades of this century.

Standing the Bible on Its Feet

In that most topsy-turvy of tales, *Alice in Wonderland*, the heroine tries to regain her perspective: from upside down to right side up, from too tall or too short to "just right." It's a complicated journey and Alice is repeatedly perplexed by those she meets along the way, those who inquire about her identity:

"Who are *you*?" said the Caterpillar.

This was not an encouraging opening for a conversation. Alice replied rather shyly, "I—I hardly know, Sir, just at present—at least I know who I *was* when I got up this morning, but I think I must have been changed several times since then."

As their conversation became more puzzling, Alice tried to get a grip on reality by remembering the stanzas:

"You are old, Father William," the young man said,
"And your hair has become very white;

5

And yet you incessantly stand on your head—
Do you think, at your age, it is right?"
"In my youth," Father William replied to his son,
"I feared it might injure the brain;
But now that I'm perfectly sure I have none,
Why I do it again and again."

The Caterpillar pronounces Alice's recital "wrong from beginning to end."

I am not about to compare the Bible to this famous adventure for children and adults, yet I do think *we* resemble Alice when it comes to finding the right perspective on the Bible. I think we are more inclined to stand the Bible, like Father William, on its head with the inevitable result that it does not make much sense either. We may not be entirely wrong from beginning to end, yet we have to stand the Bible on its feet, to look at its entire witness, before we can discern meaning from chapters and verses.

This is easier said than done. We are not accustomed to thinking about the biblical story in its totality. Readers of modern lectionaries, television evangelists, preachers, poets, and many other people are inclined to "dip into" the Bible to find a chapter, verse, line, or phrase that will open up truth, like a rabbit jumping out of a magician's hat. It is of course possible to discover ancient and abiding wisdom even from random biblical selections, but only if we are reading the book right side up.

I have three reversals in mind that pertain to ecclesiology, three ways of correcting my vision of the Bible's overall testimony about the church.

Verna Dozier first taught me that our contemporary perspective on the church is upside down. "A funny thing happened on the way to the Kingdom. The Church, the people of God, became the Church, the institution." To put this another way, we have become accustomed to interpreting the Bible as a guidebook for the religious establishment. Instead, the Bible is first of all the story of God's work and our response. It is a covenant story about the relationship between God and those chosen by God. The normative scriptural understanding of the church is as the people of God, not as an institution. In fact the Bible reveals that human inventions are secondary to the relational commandment to love God and love our neighbors as ourselves. I have nothing against religious institutions per se, they are necessary but their value depends on those they serve. Parishes, denominations, chaplaincies, religious orders, seminaries, church schools, these and other religious institutions are the means, not the ends, of the Gospel message. I still find truthfulness in the children's hand game, "Here is the church, here is the steeple, open the door and see all the people!" We need to stand the church upright on human feet, envisioning her first of all as God's people, and only secondarily as the institutional, earthen vessel that conveys us along the way. This is the biblically formative definition of ecclesiology. In the biblical narrative God's people are the essence, the formative agents of the church, not objects of religious care. To paraphrase that Walt Kelley's cartoon sage, Pogo, "We have met the church, and she is us!"

Second, the biblical record must be righted. The teaching focus of the Bible is, broadly and clearly, all humankind. By this I mean that the Bible was not intended to present role models for extraordinary saints but for ordinary people. As the contemporary ethicist Robert McAfee Brown reminds us, God's Word is for "all persons . . . no one excepted, everyone accepted." The Bible sings a song described in hymnody "of all the saints of God . . . folks like you and me." The Bible was not written to serve as a handbook for ordained ministers and other religious officials, although many seminarians are perplexed and disappointed to find that there is very little functional information on ordained ministries in the Bible. The Bible does not discuss the traditional threefold ministry of bishop, priest and deacon. The one order named there, the diaconate (1 Tim. 3: 8-13), is not described. The Greek word for deacon, *diakonos*, is applied to all people. Active service, *diakonia*, includes all those who would follow Jesus. The historical development of ordained ministries in the institutional church is largely a post-biblical story. The modern Catholic theologian, Edward Schillebeeckx, has described in several recent books on ministry how the early institutional church shifted its understanding of the Holy Spirit's gifts for ministry "from the charisma of many to a specialized charisma of just a few." With this second century shift away from the biblical understanding of empowerment in the Spirit, early patterns of ordination evolved. The forms and functions we now assign to clergy developed further in the Middle Ages and Reformation.

While the biblical record is not specifically helpful in defining ordained ministries, it does provide formative, evocative and normative expectations of the church's mission. The Bible is replete with precedents, images, stories, and theological assumptions that are foundational for understanding the church. In other words, the Bible does not speak primarily to ordained ministers—it addresses all humanity. It concentrates on building up communities of faithful people. In the Bible we, the people of God, have a larger and more definitive record than "the man called Peter."

The biblical centrality of the church, understood as God's people at work in the world, provides the context for interpreting individual ministries. Our theology of the church needs to shape our definitions of "ministry." Accordingly in the Episcopal Church's Outline of the Faith (a document traditionally called the catechism and found in the back of the 1979 Book of Common Prayer), the definition of "church" precedes that of "ministry." The church is named "the community of the New Covenant." It is the church that "carries out its mission through the ministry of all its members." Yet despite this charge I am afraid people have been encouraged to find or name their own individual ministries well before they have seriously encountered or thought much about the collective nature, mission and power of the church at work in the world. Recently, for example, I spoke with a priest who boasted of being confirmed and admitted to postulancy for Holy Orders on the same day. This priest had only limited knowledge of and experience in the Episcopal Church—for him, ministry was ordination. I think an ungrounded, literally "un-churched," theology of ministry encourages misguided aspirations for ordination, and clergy who function as "Lone Rangers" apart from the whole people of God. The Outline of the Faith reminds us that "ministry" (whether ordained or lay) is not our primary identity as people of God; Christianity is.

The people of God as a community points toward the third reversal affirmed in Scripture. Biblical language and imagery that evokes the church is usually collective, corporate, expansive and energetic, rather than individualistic, possessive or passive. Other names for the "church" include the household of God, the New Israel, a holy nation, a royal priesthood, the pillar and ground of truth, children of God, the Body of Christ, and of course the people of God, the chosen ones. In the Old Testament (which I prefer to call the Hebrew Scriptures) people understood themselves as members of a larger family, tribe and nation. In the New Testament records of the earliest Christian communities there is a formative, egalitarian ecclesiology. Those who lived in the "new creation" following upon Jesus's life, death and resurrection sought out Jew and Gentile, slave and free, male and female to give them welcome despite the ingrained hierarchies of the Roman world. There is a collective solidarity to

9

the biblical witness, a liberating power that we can still hear in early testimonies from Corinth and Galatia: "Where the spirit of the Lord is, there is liberty" and "for you were called to freedom" (2 Cor. 3: 17 and Gal. 5: 13).

I like to think of "church" as a collective reality, not as a possessive noun. I know we commonly refer to "my" church, that is, the parish to which I belong; or "my" church, often meaning "my" denomination. These are limited definitions. Even "my" individual ministry cannot truly be understood apart from the collective body of Christians. Biblical authors referred to the church in a variety of contexts, as we do. There were house communities, for example, the church in the house of Priscilla and Aquila (1 Cor. 16: 9), and groups of Christians in a given area or region, as the church in Asia Minor or Judaea. Underlying these and other referen-ces was the consciousness, established through our Jewish roots, of being part of a universal movement of those people, the *ekklesia*, called out by God. The church is *God's*; this is the correct possessive. Despite urgings of modern television evangelists, the aim of the Bible is not to invite God into our lives, but to urge us to join God's unfolding story. Robert Mc-Afee Brown corrects our understanding of the Bible, which "is not our theology but God's anthropology . . . our social ethics do not derive from who we are but from what God asks of us." We must not forget the significance of our belonging to God. This is why the church in the biblical record is fully named *laos tou theou*, the people *of God*.

In English we frequently employ diverse definitions for the same word. There is no reason to settle on only one definition for "church." The church is a building, a parish, a locality, a denomination, a worldwide communion; the church is also an institution, a socially constructed group with designated leaders and officials organized to encourage and maintain mission. The question is not what the church is, but how our understanding of the church shapes our identity as Christians. Is the church primarily an organization, or is it a people? Can it be both? If so, which understanding conveys the core, the essential ingredients of our identity?

In the biblical narrative Israel's prophets, including Jesus, customarily responded to questions not with an answer indicating exactly "what" to do, but with a psalm, a hymn, a story, or a parable that opens up new interpretations, fresh ways of thinking. There is a fable from the early Middle Ages that helps me clarify differing perspectives on the church as an institution and as God's people. I was taught this fable, "The Cathedral and the Well," by my parents. I think my mother enjoyed it because she was an actress and this fable had the requisite three acts; my father, an attorney, liked a good moral ending that was open to debate.

(Act One) The setting is a desert which, like all deserts, has to be crossed. In the middle of this desert is a well, fed by an underground spring of fresh, loud, rushing water. This particular well is fortunately located just at the point where thirsty pilgrims need refreshment if they are to survive and continue on their way. So in those days news got about that it was relatively safe to cross the desert as long as you listened for the sound of the spring and stopped to drink from the well. Generations of pilgrims were able to cross the desert and head into the wilderness—which is where God's people were usually traveling.

(Act Two) Many years later news spreads of a building in the middle of the desert, a cathedral of great beauty. Throughout the years pilgrims, when they passed, had dropped stones (some fancier than others) to mark the location of the wellspring, an improvement which they hoped would show their respect for the well. Soon a cathedral stands in the middle of this desert, one stone buttressing another. Pilgrims stop, look up and admire the cathedral from a distance. Yet most of them are close to death from thirst when they approach. They can neither hear the sounds of rushing water nor see the well, now covered by stones.

(Act Three) Centuries later, in the same desert, one very thirsty pilgrim dares to approach the cathedral, now overgrown by weeds after years of neglect. She (most late medieval pilgrims were women) notices that a stone was loose. Pulling it out, so that she might replace it correctly, she hears the sound of rushing waters! She rediscovers the well and invites her companions to drink of its life-giving waters. Soon news spreads of the cathedral *and* of the well. The cathedral was imperfectly built, always standing in need of repair; the well, which stood in its midst, is free-flowing. Future generations of pilgrims, sighting the familiar landmark of the cathedral, draw close to the well, drink of its springs, and live to cross the desert.

What of today's pilgrims? Do biblical wellsprings define our church and encourage new life? Pilgrims throughout the ages have found refreshment in the Bible, courage to cross the deserts of their own day, hope to continue in the wilderness. It is critical that each generation undertakes responsibility for passing on the story, making sure that we do not cover up the well with the magnificence of our cathedrals or with our neglect. We must still drink deeply from the wellsprings of our biblical inheritance, reading the Bible right side up, thinking about its themes.

Book of Books, Our People's Strength

I have always loved singing in church. I have favorite hymns (I suspect most people do). My mother and I would team up to reproduce a hymn. I would pay attention to and remember (in my own fashion) the lyrics; she would recall the tunes. As a child I greatly admired Percy Dearmer's hymns. Here is a favorite verse of mine, replete with clear, strong words, active verbs, and rich promises:

Book of books, our people's strength,
Statesman's, teacher's, hero's treasure,
Bringing freedom, spreading truth,
Shedding light that none can measure:
Wisdom comes to those who know thee,
All the best we have we owe thee.

Even then I changed words so I might be included, turning "statesman" into "counselor." Even now I appreciate Dearmer's optimistic, liberating theology. The "book of books" is a book of strength. It is a book for and by the people, the divinely inspired and human product of those "who toiled in thought, many diverse scrolls completing."

I like the phrase "toiled in thought," for it suggests the discipline required in adult education. We have already explored how the Bible presents the church in collective, expansive imagery. I propose to emulate Dearmer by recommending clear, strong adjectives that further impart the biblical character of the church. Five words come to mind. (There may well be others!) If I were painting the biblical landscape with a broad brush, the people of God would need to be depicted as *created*, *chosen*, *pursued*, *sent*, and *trusted*. Reflecting on these words will, I believe, allow us both to survey and portray essential biblical characteristics of the church.

The church as God's people is first of all *created*, called into life. This accords with the Greek word for church, *ekklesia*, meaning called forth, summoned, empowered, lifted up. The biblical creation story is neither detached nor impartial. It communicates God's nature, or anthropology, as well as our own. Many liberation theologians have been quick to point to God's yearning, longing for the created order. James Weldon Johnson (who also wrote lyrics for the Black anthem,

"Lift Every Voice and Sing") in *God's Trombones* portrays a creator-God who cries out, "I'm lonely . . . I'll make me a world."

> This Great God,
> Like a mammy bending over her baby,
> Kneeled down in the dust
> Toiling over a lump of clay
> Till he shaped it in his own image.

Verna Dozier similarly describes the Bible as the story of a God who creates as an act of love. The Hebrew Scriptures begin with an affirmation that we are part of God's creation. We, like our Hebrew ancestors, need to deepen our awareness of this relationship. But, Dozier emphasizes, our relationship with God is not something we have to achieve. "God has already acted for [us]."

Not only does God create a race of human beings "in our image, after our likeness," God also shares with human beings responsibility for the created order; in the cosmologies of the ancient Near East this was the domain of other gods (see Gen. 1: 26-32). One day as I read the creation stories, it dawned on me that in receiving dominion over the fish of the sea, for example, human beings replaced Neptune and other classical deities. From the beginning God gives authority, "dominion," charging humanity with serious obligations for the earth. The Jewish mystic and ethicist, Rabbi Abraham Joshua Heschel, interprets the creation story as establishing God's need for humanity. In Genesis God calls us to join in working toward the further realization of creation. By describing the church as God's *created* people, from the beginning we acknowledge God's work and ours.

This theme of accountability is repeated in the description of the church as God's *chosen* people. God's promise to Abraham, Sarah and their descendants is one of adoption, a unique relationship emphasizing that Yahweh is Israel's God and that Israel is Yahweh's people. The choice of this small tribe does not rest on Israel's ethnic identity, as we might think. Harvey Guthrie reminds us that biblical Israel was a trans-tribal reality with a multi-ethnic identity. The unique character of God's choice depends on the covenant, a specific biblical declaration of continuing identity and promise. This divine act of election commences with declaring God's identity as the one "who brought you out of the land of Egypt, out of the house of bondage" (Ex. 20: 1, see also Deut. 5: 6). The Exodus story is the paradigm for the Hebrew Scriptures; it establishes the pattern of God's mighty acts remembered and promised. In the covenant Israel promises to be monotheistic, to have and to worship only one god, Yahweh, and to behave in accord with this commitment. The covenant provides the basis for what follows as the people of Israel labor, not always successfully, to live out the identity of God's chosen people.

The choice of Israel as a particular people to praise Yahweh is a point of departure in the biblical narrative. God repeatedly reminds Israel that it is to "bring everyone," even outsiders, to call upon Yahweh's name (Is. 43: 1-13). The identity of Israel is a locus, not a restriction. The so-called Old Covenant of the Hebrew people is further extended in the early Christian affirmation of a New Covenant community that welcomes Gentiles as well as Jews. God's chosen people have a biblically collective and expanding identity. Christians are incorporated into this identity in baptism following the New Covenant commitment to God as revealed in Christ Jesus. This way of thinking about baptism emphasizes the choice of a Christian identity that is stronger than all social and historical oppositions within the community of believers, an identity that overcomes all prior classifications. The community of the New Covenant embodies

the more universalized identity of a church incarnate of
many peoples chosen by God.

Thankfully the biblical church is also *pursued* by God. As
a lawyer's daughter I know of the human tendency to interpret contracts diversely. The law helps us do just that. I
would be less optimistic about the legacy of the biblical
church were it not that the God of the biblical narrative is
relentlessly in pursuit. I find comfort in God's resolve to
track us down despite repeated transgressions.

Let me paraphrase some of this biblical record. A small,
unimportant group of tribes, although honored and reas-
sured as God's chosen people, constantly falters as it tries to
live under the covenant. Again and again Israel stumbles, in
spite of God's Word. She almost learns to enjoy the exile by
refusing to listen to God's appointed leaders, by raising up
kings of her own making, by neglecting prophets sent to contend with her kings, in other words, by breaking the covenant
in giving authority to other gods. When the people of Israel
receive the gift of God's own Son, the culmination of God's
biblically redemptive acts, even then they choose to follow
Caesar, not the Messiah. Then the Holy Spirit is sent to pursue us, again and again, an advocate for our transgression in
this world. It is significant that the New Testament does not
stop after the four gospels, but follows the people of the
church into the Book of Acts and beyond, telling the story of
God's abiding presence in the events of this people's history.

God remains close to the people. This is a listening and
responding God, a living God that dwells in the thick of
things, the risk-taking God of Abraham, Isaac, Jacob, Peter,
Paul, Sarah, Leah, Rachel, Mary Magdalene and the "woman
bent double" (Lk. 13: 10-16). The ongoing biblical account of
God's liberating activity reveals a God of intimacy. "Our
Father who art in heaven" is very close, the one who is always present. God takes sides, standing with Israel in out-

lasting Egypt, Babylon, its own kings, the Assyrians and other disasters. Biblical faith is distinct from other world religions in its emphasis on the continuing presence of God in the worldly affairs of human history. This pursuing God works through the power of love that is not just rooted in the past, but seeks new life in the future. The prophet Micah insists that we "walk humbly with God" (Mic. 6: 8). God's assurance in the giving of the covenant is one of presence, walking with us, pursuing us despite our rebuffs along the way.

In the biblical record the church is *sent*, commissioned to go into the world. The world is the church's working place. This is not the usual message of television evangelists or of religious sects that try to separate their members from the world, as if protected in a plastic bubble from contagious values. I find it ironic that persons with anti-world perspectives display large signs at sports events advertising "John 3: 16," a text which insistently grounds ecclesiology in this world: "For God so *loved the world* that he gave his only Son, that whosoever believes in him should not perish but have eternal life. For God *sent the Son into the world, not to condemn the world, but that the world might be saved through him*" (John 3: 16-17, emph. added).

The entire biblical record is filled with God's calling and sending. The Gospel of Matthew concludes with the Great Commission, sending disciples to "all nations" (Matt. 28: 16-20). In the Gospel of John the risen Jesus encourages his disciples to continue their work, "as the Father has sent me, even so I send you" (John 20: 21). Paul writes, "In Christ, God was reconciling the world unto himself" (2 Cor. 5: 19). The Bible speaks about our lives on *earth*, a word that occurs many more times than "heaven." In Paul's ecclesiology early Christian communities become the continuing locus of God's presence on earth. The church both in divine example and in biblical image is world-centered. Kraemer describes the church as "the community of the *sent*." It exists on behalf of the world.

The biblical church is created, chosen, pursued, sent and *trusted*. By trusted I mean "given an important task to do," empowered to work. The central mission is not preservation, nor restoration, nor building reservations of Christian people who can live in the midst of unfriendly territory. The biblical mission of the church is to be God's agents in the world. One of my favorite passages from Isaiah begins "Listen to me, O coastlands, and hearken, you peoples from afar" and declares Israel's God-given mission:

> It is too light a thing that you
> should be my servant,
> to raise up the tribes of Jacob
> and to restore the preserved of
> Israel;
> I will give you as a light to the
> nations,
> that my salvation may reach to
> the end of the earth (Is. 49: 1, 6).

In this testimony the people's work is more than that of continuing the lineage of Abraham and Sarah; this is expected but it is "too light a thing" by itself. Israel is charged with being a trusted agent, a public sign and symbol to others, "a light to the nations" that salvation is found in God. This missionary journey will extend the people of God "to the end of the earth." If the church must choose between church maintenance and mission to the nations, God entrusts us with the latter, foundational responsibility. This is a salvific mission, representing God in Christ on earth. The "book of books" portrays the human church as divinely created and repeatedly chosen, pursued, sent, and trusted in mission.

There is one serious provisional note to this mighty biblical legacy. It is a realistic note that cautions against pride and overweening zeal. Isaiah describes Israel as *a* light, *a* sign, not *the* light, *the* sign. This should be reassuring news. The church is not God on earth, but God's trusted people on earth. St. Augustine supposedly said, "God has many the church does not have. The church has many God does not have!" The church is provisional, here to provide. It is not definitive. Communities of the Old and the New Covenants struggled with the perceived tension between zeal for the church's mission and openness to others. The church has erred and may err again. Biblical ecclesiology rests on Yahweh's people being called into a special partnership with God. The strength of the covenant rests not in the equality of this relationship, but in divine assurance of the historical and ongoing account of God's liberating activity. The most famous neo-orthodox theologian of this century, Karl Barth, revealed biblically sound ecclesiology when, it is said, he introduced a sermon: "I have three points in mind this morning. First, God is omnipotent—all-powerful. Second, God is omniscient—all-knowing. Third, now some random thoughts on baptism." The biblical church is shaped by God's mighty works and our covenanted responsibilities as baptized Christians.

Inviting Ourselves into God's Story

I hold a personal remembrance of a particular Bible which was prominently placed on my mother's bedside table. Bits of paper, occasional photos of friends and family, pieces of dried palm leaves, a delicately crocheted cross (intended to be a book mark yet unequal to the task of marking several places at once), a letter from my grandmother bestowing a Seth Thomas clock, marginal notes in my mother's unmistakable hand (barely legible but "full of character," she said), exclamation points and question marks: these treasures and more awaited those who explored this book. This Bible was both literally and figuratively stuffed with meaning. It was a favored place to collect additional stories, current questions and cherished memories. It was a resource that provided, in words from a famous English Reformation collect for the Bible, "the patience and comfort of thy Holy Word." I regard the Bible as an inheritance that connects me with a mother long dead and with generations of ancestors known and unknown.

In the closing section of this chapter I want to explore and identify several strategies that can help adults learn more about the Bible and about their faith in general. I chose the method of sharing a family story initially because the Bible is part of my genealogy, both as *this* book and as *the* book. Whether we bring our personal, familial history or other recollections to the Bible, it is inevitable that we read about the past through the personal prisms of our own lives.

The value of education increases when we allow ourselves to become part of the conversation. My recollections are different from yours! I share them to encourage and invite your own reflections. Unless we bring our experiences to learning, education will remain disconnected, pertinent only to others. It is important that we start with ourselves, begin with our experiences, and ask our questions. This is not only a humanly sensitive way to invest education with deeper worth, it accords with biblical theology. The definitive New Testament insight and instruction was the Incarnation. The advent of God dwelling in common human history carries the biblical promise for post-resurrection Christians that God continues to dwell in us and we in God.

In a later chapter I will explore how the Incarnation radically shapes Christian theology. Educationally I want to emphasize that by virtue of the Incarnation, our lives carry news of the Gospel. We are, in the words of the prophetic lawyer and theologian William Stringfellow, "each one of us parables." We may not always discern the meaning, or several meanings, of our local stories. The point is that we are summoned to bring our testimonies, like generations of Jewish and Christian ancestors, to the ongoing process of carrying on God's work in the world. Inviting ourselves into God's story will help us read the Bible more effectively.

For the sake of a healthy, broadly informed church it is important that members share in the responsibility for learning more about the Bible. Stringfellow believed, quite correctly, that neglect of Bible study in our parishes has led to "nothing less than the denigration of the laity." When the gifts of any group in the body of Christ are not esteemed, when we act as if a seminary education is required for learning about the Bible (as though it represented some static body of theory open only to scholars), when laity are reduced to spectators in worship with only token appearances, when rules and other assumptions keep people from the Bible, I wonder who we are trying to protect. Surely not the Bible. Since the biblical church includes us all, we've no need to protect the church. I don't think most clergy want to be educationally isolated from others who seek to know the Word of God. Responsibility for biblical literacy rests with us all. It is a cultural problem.

Some time ago I heard a Public Radio commentator remark that the Bible is one of the three most quoted books in America (along with Karl Marx's *Communist Manifesto* and Adam Smith's *Wealth of Nations*) that has not been read by those who quote it. It is as if the people of God have been engaged in a prolonged fit of inattention since the Reformation returned the Bible to the people. I suppose many lay persons think learning the Bible is someone else's role.

Complacency with established roles and patterns is only one biblical sin from which many of us need liberation.

I am disturbed about the overall implications of shallow standards for biblical education in a congregation. If clergy and a few other leaders are the only ones regularly reading or studying the Bible, then a parish's listening skills and identity as a people in mission are limited. When a congregation does not reflect biblically on the everyday lives of its parishioners, then its collective wisdom is impoverished. When professional clerical perspectives are unchallenged by other visions and perceptions, parochial needs may be over-emphasized to the neglect of the church's work in the world. The mission of the whole church is impoverished by biblical illiteracy. Adult biblical education is a necessity not a luxury. Most of us require ongoing communication and nurture to carry out our Christian identity in the world. We can no longer depend, if we ever could, on a learned clergy.

Teaching was a chief biblical preoccupation. Instruction in the faith was extended to new members. During the first five centuries after Christ, group instruction involved inquirers (catechumens) who studied and prayed for up to three years before admission to the sacraments. Initiation was not the only occasion for learning. Teaching took place through the interpretation of the Hebrew Scriptures, through preaching, through passing on oral sayings, through making public confessions, and through the daily ethical struggle to live as covenanted people. Paul said, "Let all things be done for edification" (1 Cor. 14: 26). The biblical aim of education was building up the community. Parents were responsible for teaching children and adult education was not optional. This is clear in Paul's pointed question, "You then who teach others, will you not teach yourself?" (Rom. 2: 21)

The Bible has a convincing history of collective liberation as well as individual transformation. Bible study has traditionally been a group undertaking. Only in cultures and among classes with increased material wealth have more than a handful of individuals owned Bibles. Recourse to the Bible has proven essential in resisting oppression. It was used in World War II by the anti-Nazi Resistance, by Jews and Christians imprisoned during the Holocaust, by teams of civil rights workers in North America, and by those who continue the struggle against apartheid in South Africa's Black "homelands." Today the Bible is being heard and interpreted anew by local groups of lay people in Latin America's "base communities" (*communidades eclesiales de base*).

One essential guideline for collective study of the Bible is the need to take both the Bible and group members seriously. Hearing the Word of God, in the past and in the present, is related to hearing one another. Careful listening to the Word of God and to the words of one another can result in enriched insight and powerful solidarity. Groups, as well as individuals, bring distinct identities to the Bible. When a group is self-aware and self-critical it can claim wisdom born out of its own context and point to its wider mission. A small group is like a church; it is a means, not an end. Groups that build tabernacles to their own vision have learned only to listen to one another. Groups grow in wisdom when they become aware of their own contexts, limitations and advantages.

The Bible notices human contexts. It considers the ground on which its witnesses stand. Want and abundance, geographical location, class strata, previous history, these and other factors shape the meaning of a story, parable or psalm. The rich young man and the woman at the well raise and pose different problems, though both point toward discipleship (Matt. 19: 16-22 and John 4: 5-42). Biblical truth is conveyed diversely. Our social location influences the way we read the Bible. In adult education truth is often plural. No one has *the* corner on truth. Our vision may be limited by what we can see for ourselves. Truth is larger than an author and her readers, a preacher and his congregation. Truth is something that happens among us.

I know this in a personal way because I have a twin brother. As "twins" we grew up in the glare of comparisons between men and women, between different ways of learning, different preferences and different vocations. Although we were raised in the same household and had many similar experiences, we usually reached different conclusions. I used to think that we learned patience; now I know we learned that fortitude and genuine diversity are valuable companions.

I assume that serious disagreement and anger are inevitable components of education. Even Moses confronted God in anger, complaining that the people expected too much of him (Num. 11: 10-12). Elizabeth Cady Stanton once said, "There is no use saying what people are ready to hear." A famous fourth- century preacher and bishop whose name meant "mouth of gold," John Chrysostom, remarked, "Whoever is without anger when there is cause for anger, sins." I am angered (and I believe legitimately) by widespread misappropriations of biblical revelation. The Bible is not a legal reference book of "right" answers to given questions, nor is it a weapon that entitles us to condemn others. These applications of God's life-giving Word make me even more determined to use the Bible to free it from the bonds in which we have it imprisoned. The overall character of the Bible testifies to a living God who offers assurance, not rules. The more I reflect on biblical themes, the more I discover that it is powerfully exemplary, not narrowly legislative.

Finally, I am convinced that in adult education, advanced is not perfect. My favorite cartoon character Pogo once offered a motto for students of all ages, "We have faults which we have hardly used up yet." Orderliness, certainty, fastidious logic, perfection, immobility . . . these and other characteristics are seldom human and certainly not biblical virtues. The Bible does not have to lie about human nature. Moreover, the Bible displays the ethos of a Hebraic world accustomed to change and movement, not a Hellenistic world seeking order and control. In Scripture, theology is in motion. The Spirit moves across the land, enlivening God's people. The Bible releases and reverses our most cherished assumptions; it turns from the culturally powerful and listens to those on the underside. The Bible, in Robert McAfee Brown's phrase, brings "unexpected news."

This is one reason why I think the simplest, least erudite, methods of study are often best for adult inquirers. We need to stay close to the text. I find scholarly commentaries and other exegetical works interesting, helpful and at times amusing. I do not think they are required tools for study. Sometimes other persons' knowledge can get in the way of our learning. Listen to the Bible as it is read, reflect on it in groups, read whole chapters and sections regularly. Be willing to question what biblical witnesses are saying to us, bring your own questions, and learn with others.

Remember the Bible is the people's book. It may be a companion in individual transformation, but it was not designed to elicit individualized messages. Instead of searching for minute applications, try working from the image or vision revealed in Scripture toward your responses. The Bible actually points beyond itself toward the unfolding of a better history. It is like a parable, a teaching tool with many layers that clarifies obedience but not specific applications, inviting comparison with the common history of our own lives. The

Bible offers the people of God assurance that God has acted for us. It calls us, as it did our ancestors, to belong to a biblical people who celebrate God's ongoing work and our continuing response.

LOOKING BACKWARD, THINKING FORWARD

Remembering the People

Memory can be a powerful ally, history a useful friend. In the midst of the Second World War, T. S. Eliot in his poem "Little Gidding" proclaimed that the use of memory is for human freedom, "liberation from the future as well as the past." For Eliot, who wrote the *Four Quartets* during the Second World War, history was a theological companion which had the power to free us even in the midst of conflagration and despair.

Another document which comes to us from the wartime event that changed the course of history is a prayer written by a condemned Jew in Belsen:

> O God, remember not only the men and women of good will, but also those of ill will. But do not only remember all the suffering they have inflicted on us. Remember the fruits we bought thanks to this suffering: our comradeship, our loyalty, our humility, our courage, our generosity, the greatness of heart that has grown out of all of this. And when they come to

judgement, let all the fruits that we have borne be their forgiveness.

Remembering, as in this prayer, can bring perspective andbuild tolerance among peoples. Remembering is drawing energy from past events, both good and evil. Through our memories we can convert understanding of past events into insight that illumines our future. Remembering is about looking back in order to think ahead.

Mark Gibbs was an energetic English champion of lay ministries who worked after the Second World War to educate laity throughout Europe and North America. He often said that Christian laity do not really know much about their past. Gibbs believed that we already had the biblical theology we needed; what we lacked was the historical courage to go out into the world as Christians and do the work we are given to do. I think that as laity not only do we lack a history, but that the history with which we are usually provided is neither useful nor liberating. I am reminded of my college western civilization course which focused upon generals, wars and conquests; or the numerous parish church history lectures (some of which I've given) emphasizing bishops, councils and cathedrals. In neither case were ordinary people central to the story, nor were they easy to find. We can find institutional histories and biographies of great men and women, but where do we look to find humanity? What are models, organizing principles, helpful questions, the useful images for thinking about laypersons? How can we think about and envision the road ahead if we cannot see those who have gone on before?

I have come to find encouragement in the testimonies of lay persons throughout the centuries. Learning about the distinct contributions of lay men and women is for me like discovering legacies from a family tree. It is illuminating to know about earlier generations. Yet as a young student, I must admit that the study of history was a chore. Along with many others, I had a "bad history" with history as I struggled to remember all those dates and names. I was delighted to discover that one of my favorite authors, Jane Austen, found history tiresome, too. In *Northanger Abbey* she characterizes it as "the quarrels of popes and kings, with wars or pestilences in every page; the men all so good for nothing, and hardly any women at all." I now know that we cannot force-feed data into students of any age. Besides, as anyone who tries to keep a checkbook balance knows, we do not have to remember the things we can look up. This is good news for amateur and professional historians alike.

Memory is an ally; it stores what is of meaning to us. I have a terrible memory for the casual details of daily living. Yet my love of history, and consequently my memory of selected events, comes from recovering stories of ordinary women and men. Each year images of people who lived during the English Reformation, my own field of scholarship for historical research, become clearer and more populous. When I refer to "doing history," I simply mean the sensitive depiction of historical peoples so that those of us in later generations may derive insight from their experience. This process has rich theological value. History frees us from a past that was never fixed. The contemporary liberation theologian, Gustavo Gutierrez insists that the history and traditions of the church are our heritage, not our boundaries. When we look at what really happened, indeed, at several often contradictory things that occurred simultaneously, we discover that life in past centuries was no simpler, nor any less confused, than the present. History is about traditions, in the plural. This is good news: positive, progressive realities exist alongside suffering, endurance and confusion. Testimonies from our ancestors, like stories from the Bible, open up traditional knowledge so that we may learn from the past.

I am also convinced that the knowledge of history is helpful because it exposes our preoccupation with present-mindedness. It gives us a way to test our arrogance. Each generation has a way of thinking it is the best, or the worst! History can provide safeguards against over-confidence in this age's wisdom as well as counsels against despair. There is value in learning humility from the struggles and achievements of those who have gone before us. By exploring what happened within the social contexts of the earlier centuries, we can realize anew the necessity of examining today's problems within their own contexts. Then as now, we will find collective, corporate images. The history of Christianity is largely an inter-generational and multi-generational story inhabited by groups of people living and working together.

Knowledge of history also assists us in moving from the present into the future. The Reformation scholar, Jane Demsey Douglas, describes the historian as a person who backs up a thousand years or so to get a running start on the questions at hand. We are all familiar with the phrase, "We've never done it that way before!" Perhaps yes, perhaps no. In any event knowledge of history unfailingly provides evidence for change. Indeed the process of reclaiming the history of any particular group (culture, ethnic community, race, class or gender) is in itself a vehicle for change. When we want to set goals for the future, whether in corporate America or local congregations, we can look to lessons from the immediate past. The process of research, retelling, reinterpreting history allows new visions to emerge. Re-visioning enlarges our ability to imagine different futures. Looking backward helps us think forward.

Most of what traditionally passes for church history is documentation of the framework, building, ordering, bureaucratic development, and other institutional support for the church as an organization. "Great" individuals like King Henry VIII, Thomas More or Queen Elizabeth I are singled out almost exclusively for their contributions to social institutions; the rest of the people in the story are usually accorded minority status. As the caterpillar pointed out to Alice—to use one of the stories with which this book began— "this is wrong from beginning to end." As with the Bible, somehow we have to stand history back on ordinary human feet and look at the entire witness, before we can discern meaning from this or that historical event.

However interesting institutional church history may or may not be, it is not the central story of Christian peoples. This chapter is intended to correct some of the negative images and impressions suggested by books like Anne Rowthorn's *The Liberation of the Laity*, which suggests that the laity has always, or more often than not, been choked off from real participation in the church. Frankly, the great-men-great-institutions way of seeing history is not only erroneous, but harmful. It breeds apathy and distances us from the heritage of our ancestors' generous and energetic religious commitments.

In this chapter I wish to highlight moments from our Christian ancestors' lives that have to do with the rest of the people in the story. I want to show the people of God as a great cloud of witnesses across the generations. These historical moments show a reversal in which the laity, the majority, find their voices. From this perspective, the furthering of the institutional church is only one part of the story. This perspective calls for patient listening and careful historical reconstruction. There have been times when it is hard to hear the voices of ordinary people, times when those with less-than-great status have been silenced, ignored or trivialized. In this story women, usually the largest demographic group in Western European and North American churches, naturally play more prominent roles as leaders and contributors. When we look at the wider picture, laity come to light as participants and change-makers rather than as passive recipients of official edicts.

The dominant, pivotal themes of the larger story are renewal, education and mission: lifelines of Christian history. New Testament records, particularly the Book of Acts, depict early Christian communities which expressed the dream and reality of laity whom God empowered for mission and service. I want to look at three other times (although there are more than three) in the long history of Christianity which present a similar picture. As an Anglican and thus part of a church established during the Protestant Reformation, I am interested in re-envisioning this period of reform and renewal from the perspective of ordinary men and women. As an American Christian, I have inherited a religious culture shaped by the great lay missionary movements of the nineteenth century, and I need to know this legacy better. As a Christian citizen living in the closing decades of a century marked by genocide and the threat of nuclear warfare, I know that it is critical to inquire about the lessons that grew out of lay activism during and after the Second World War. I wonder too what models, what insights, these three historical experiences—religious reformation in sixteenth-century England, expansion of religious activity in nineteenth-century North America, and the construction of new Christian organizations following the Second World War—hold for us as we approach the twenty-first century?

People of the Book

As any viewer of Masterpiece Theater 1
and his six wives represent intriguing, c
casionally horrifying subjects for histori
Popular histories of the Reformation ha
focused on this egotistical king. Other great n
not in girth) like Martin Luther, John Calvin   ...us
Loyola provide abundant biographical copy fo1 ...iose interested in the founders of religious groups. Indeed the reform
of religion during the 1500s in Europe and England is
generally presented as if the ideas and actions of a few great
men changed habitual religious practices overnight. Here is
yet another reversal. These leaders were undeniably influential, yet to keep the focus on them is to caricature a complex,
revolutionary process. Instead I choose to focus on those
revolutionary innovations which, when considered together,
can be said to have reformed and renewed, as if by spontaneous combustion, many of the ways people practiced
their faith.

At the heart of the Protestant Reformation, in all of what
we would later call its denominational branches, is the right
of individuals and groups to listen and speak to God directly. This principle of divine accessibility is the central inheritance of all reformed religions. It is accurate to describe
the long-term impact of the several revolutionary components of the Reformation as the triumph of the laity's right
to know—to know God better by having direct access to the
formative resources of their faith. Consequently, one of the
most significant changes had to do with the way information
spreads. Those of us who live in a computer culture should
not be surprised to learn of the radical transformation caused
by technological alterations in communication. The fif-
teenth-century invention of moveable type for printing presses shaped and changed the nature of the entire culture. The
move from a handwritten to a "print" culture meant that vir-

tually anyone who could read had access to religious authorities and discourse.

The Reformation in Europe and in England was the first mass movement to take advantage of increasingly available and inexpensive printed texts. Laity and clergy, rich and poor, rural and urban, learned and uneducated, women and men . . . by no means could all of them read, but most could be read to. Access to information gives power, and most Reformation theologians wanted the Bible to be widely dispersed among the people. Yet this attitude was not shared by Roman Catholic officials. In hierarchical churches, where decision-making is restricted to bishops or cardinals, access to information and influence are controlled and distributed according to status. Perhaps accurately, English reformers believed that one of the reasons Roman Catholic hierarchy had prevailed for so long was because most laity, without access to written sources of the faith, were influenced primarily by visual images—statues, relics, paintings—rather than by books. A poor, aged widow testified in 1556 that her faith in the age of Henry VIII was a "dead faith . . . because she did not then understand what she did believe." Accordingly English reformers labored to remove any official or practical prohibitions on reading the Bible. They proclaimed the printing press as "God's own miracle," a blessing for all and a weapon for combating error.

A second revolutionary achievement was the translation of the Bible from Latin, Greek and Hebrew texts into vernacular, the common languages of Western Europe. Previously only the aristocracy, who could afford expensive manuscripts, and the better-educated clergy had access to biblical manuscripts. The appearance of printed English bibles in the 1530s was so revolutionary—because it challenged set ideas about who could read what—that at first their distribution was forbidden, and then limited by the state to the upper classes. Eventually, when parish churches were required to provide the English Bible for the use of their congregations, such bibles had to be chained to lecterns lest they be stolen.

The complete biblical text was expensive. Members of the young printing trade soon benefited by publishing short selections from the Bible. Editions of the Psalter, the epistles, various books of the New Testament and biblically-based devotional manuals were popular and could be obtained by all but the poor. The price of one of these small books, which could be carried in your pocket—hence the name "pocket book"—was equivalent to feeding a family for one or two weeks. The Bible was a best-seller, a valued possession worth saving for and passing on to a family member or friend in your will. By the end of the sixteenth century, reading and hearing the Bible read was a highly popular form of recreation among many men and women.

Actually many pre-Reformation Christians were biblically literate, their faith was permeated by the visually rich scriptural textures of late medieval Catholicism. Reformers, who anticipated how popular reading and hearing the Bible would be, distributed these vernacular books with tremendous enthusiasm and idealism. These reformers envisioned the Bible as an authority that would encourage uniformity of belief among all sorts and conditions of women and men. In this regard they were at best naive. Thomas Cranmer, Henry VIII's Archbishop of Canterbury, wrote in his 1540 Preface to the "Great Bible"—so named because it was so large—that all classes, including women, could learn from Scripture:

> The Holy Ghost hath so ordered and attempered [sic] the scriptures, that in them as well publicans, fishers, and shepherds may find their edification, as great doctors [professors] their erudition . . . . the prophets and apostles wrote their books so that their special in-

tent and purpose might be understood and perceived of every reader.

What a far cry is this vision of shared understanding from contemporary battles over interpreting the Bible! Yet it gave way to a diversity of biblically-based faiths that developed out of the Reformation—Lutherans, Presbyterians, Baptists, and Anglicans. We should not be surprised that debates about the meaning of biblical passages continue today throughout popular as well as scholarly communities. This is an inherent Protestant legacy which the Reformation fueled with the widespread distribution of vernacular bibles.

The laity's growing familiarity with biblical texts changed in its turn some of the fundamental assumptions about authority. By the Latin phrase *sola scriptura* ("Scripture alone") Protestant reformers had emphasized the primary authority of the Bible for Christian living. Not only were all things necessary for salvation (that is, all essential doctrines) contained in Scripture, but the Bible itself was to be the primary authority for ascertaining faithful religious practices. Martin Luther, for example, cited the Bible to prove that papal approval of the sale of indulgences (pardons granted in advance of committing sins) was scandalous. Furthermore Luther argued that the papacy had "captured" the Bible by claiming to be the sole arbiter of biblical interpretation and by insisting that the Pope as Christ's vicar on earth was head of all Christendom. Accordingly each of the reformed churches "protesting" papal rule, which is the origin of the name "Protestant," worked out its own stance for dispersing the authority of biblical interpretation throughout the community.

What did this theological revolution in the warrants for belief have to do with the practice of religion among ordinary people? A good deal. We cannot document why or when people changed their inner beliefs other than by pointing to alterations in their external behavior. Gradually many people turned away from traditional Roman Catholic practices, those "works of faith" which were customary among pre-Reformation Catholics: going on a pilgrimage, making a private confession and seeking priestly absolution, endowing masses to be said for the dead, observing a local saint's day or a village patronal feast. Practices which Protestant reformers considered unbiblical, as well as superstitious, were suppressed, which put an end to the veneration of relics, amulets, or statues, as well as a plethora of benefits reputedly gained from consecrated bread. These and other habitual aspects of the rich devotional vocabulary of Roman Catholicism were replaced by increased reading, memorization, and study of the Bible. Hearing sermons became, next to bear-baiting, the most popular outdoor activity. In the famous London preaching station, called Paul's Cross because it stood in front of St. Paul's Church, a two-hour glass reminded zealous preachers of their maximum length of sermons. These and other measures for imbibing the Bible revealed the fact that the populace in general agreed with the basic Protestant affirmation of the power of God's Word, as opposed to the magical intervention of priests.

Reformation insistence on the authority of the Bible meant that the routines of parish worship itself had to change. In England, vernacular bibles influenced preparation of the service manual we now call the Book of Common Prayer. Most traditional historical and liturgical scholarship has described these Tudor prayer books as "change agents." From the perspective of the laity, however, this is erroneous. Habitual turning to biblical warrants for belief and practice, indeed the biblically-inspired atmosphere of the Reformation, were more consequential for change than prayer book worship. This is clear in the testimonies of simple, rural people who suffered for their reformed faith during the reign of the Roman Catholic queen, Mary Tudor, or "Bloody Mary." It was God's Word, "the Scripture-Book" and *not* the Prayer Book, for which they were willing to suffer and, if necessary, accept martyrdom. When a farmer's daughter was challenged on the source of her theological understanding, she replied: "I have (I thank God) read God's book." When pressed by her examiner, "Why what manner of book [do] thee call God's book?", she replied, "It is the New Testament. What call you it?!" Another woman, a miller's wife, was characterized as "thick of hearing" yet "quick in understanding" God's Word. The Bible was an agent and companion in conversion. Few laity would have thought of owning a Prayer Book. When Anglicans are described as "people of the Book," it is historically more accurate to assume that the Bible is what is meant here and not the Prayer Book.

Patterns of worship were tailored to biblical principles. Thomas Cranmer, the primary author of the first Books of Common Prayer, crafted these books to provide access to the Bible. With the contemporary appetite for reading the Bible in mind, he assigned lengthy sections, often whole chapters, to be read at daily offices and Sunday services. Sunday lessons were printed in the Prayer Book for all to see, and this significant addition continued through the 1928 American Book of Common Prayer. In Tudor England the reformed lectionary allowed the laity to hear and to read the Psalter once a month, most of the Hebrew Scriptures annually, and the New Testament three times a year. Regular preaching was required by the Prayer Book, with sermons provided in books of homilies for those clergy who were unable to preach. Such clergy, in the popular parlance of the day, were called unsympathetically "dumb dogs." The central biblical sacraments were dramatized in the services of baptism and Eucharist. The entire service was printed in English, including those stage directions called rubrics, noting who is to do what next. Participation was the main thing, symbolic of the laity's right to know what was going on in worship.

Laity were vital in generating a fifth revolution, one seldom mentioned in conventional history books. Their search for biblical literacy in its turn expanded the social boundaries of education in general. Officially the Prayer Book's only educational requirement was memorizing the catechism, a formal question-and-answer examination by the local minister on the Ten Commandments, Apostles' Creed, and Lord's Prayer. Many members of the newly reformed faith, however, demanded more. They brought Christian education into their homes; instead of parish churches, these settings became the real centers of religious education. Many women, most of them without access to formal schooling, taught themselves to read with the Bible as their primary text. Mothers passed on this education to children and servants, while fathers recorded buying a "first Bible" for a child. Parents noted in their diaries the progress of their children's awareness of the faith. Even the way people talked about the Bible began to change, with nurturing phrases becoming commonplace: Cranmer called the Bible "the pap of God's Holy Word." Other images about nurture became commonplace. Domestic handbooks for parents appeared instructing them to teach their children the Bible "like skillful nurses," feeding neither too much nor too little at a time, but instead following children's natural appetites.

Even more striking was the fact that there was no official church plan or guide for domestic education. Parish life simply became more dependent on the home. By the end of the sixteenth century, treatises were written describing households as centers of the faith, seminaries and even "little churches" of God. One historian has described the overall impact of the Reformation in England as the "spiritualization of the household."

From the perspective of the people, the Reformation is the story of the converting influences not of "great men" but of "great books." The Bible in English, not Henry VIII, deserves to be called the "founder" of the reformed Church in England. With direct access to the sources of their religion, in English bibles and prayer books, lay people no longer depended upon learned elites or priests' intercessions. The English Reformation in many respects depended upon the cooperation and enthusiasm of laypersons. With bibles on their laps and prayer books in the pews, women and men took over the work of Christian education. When we speak about our Protestant inheritance, the primary legacies are a biblically reformed faith, worship in English according to the Prayer Book, and a much wider knowledge of Scripture.

"I Must Be Up and Doing!"

Most of us grew up knowing the church as a social structure; the church was to be found in buildings and in a hierarchy of officials. Yet those early Christians whose lives are chronicled in the Book of Acts encountered the church as a community; the biblical "church" was embodied in the lives of God's chosen people. Our nineteenth-century American ancestors knew the church as active commitment to mission; the church was to be found among groups and movements connecting individual and personal piety with the zeal for social reform. The church meant group activity, outdoor meetings, lobbying for education, caring for those in need, lecturing statesmen on abolition, moral reform, suffrage and prohibition. The true "old-time religion" of my maternal grandmother—who was proud to be related to the popular late nineteenth-century revivalist Dwight Lyman Moody—was grounded in the domestic piety of her home, yet forcefully aimed toward the community and the world. There was very little that was peaceful, passive, apolitical, or even parochial about this matriarch and her cohorts.

The nineteenth century was a great age for the laity. People did not talk about lay ministry; they did it. Nineteenth-century Protestants independently expanded the witness, nature and shape of religion in North America. Neither the Puritans nor any other of our colonial ancestors made America a Christian nation. In 1860 when Abraham Lincoln became President, only one in seven Americans were church members, a smaller proportion than in any other Christian country. Look at these statistics: in 1810, only 18% of American people were church adherents; by the end of the century this number had just about tripled to 51%. In this century church membership rates have continued to rise, reaching 62% in the most recent estimate of 1980. Even to an anti-statistical person like myself, these dramatic increases in church membership become even more remarkable given overall growth in this nation's population: from about 9 million in 1820, to over 75 million in 1900, up to 245 million in 1985. The overall trend is clear. We have a surprisingly long and steady history of increasing church membership. This history was established and shaped by an enthusiastic outpouring of lay missionary activity.

What fueled this extraordinary expansion of religion in America? Why were these folks able to accomplish so much? I want to peruse these questions by focusing on several areas of lay achievement.

I am not entirely sure why nineteenth-century American religion was fundamentally activist. One thing was clear: women were the central instigators and architects of religion in this century. Modern historians have only recently discovered this "surprising" and predominant feature. My maternal grandmother, however, would not have been surprised. There is overwhelming evidence that the energies and activities of nineteenth-century women shaped the character of American Christianity whether as leaders of humanitarian enterprises, influential literary figures, founders of religious groups, or political and ecclesiastical agitators for reform. As noted in the memoir of one woman from a frontier Missouri town, "[Women] simply saw and knew what had to be done, and did it, or it wouldn't have been done." By the end of the century the black educator, suffragist, and reformer—Anna Julia Cooper—underscored the importance of women's work as "missionary agents":

> The earnest well trained Christian young woman, as a teacher, as homemaker, as wife, mother, or silent influence even, is as potent a missionary agent among our people as is the theologian; and I claim that at the present stage of our development in the South she is more important and necessary.

A significant and enduring part of this cultural shift in nineteenth-century American religion was tonal. An atmosphere of sentimentality replaced harsher Puritan mores and theology. In the ever-popular literary magazines of the day, women, especially mothers, were acclaimed moral "guardians" of America's civic virtue. They were charged with inculcating the so-called feminine virtues of piety, purity, obedience and domesticity. Women's particular duty was to instill these values, ensuring their survival amid a booming industrial society marked by commercial competition and aggressive capitalism. Even conventional historians accept the thesis which literary historian Ann Douglas presents in *The Feminization of American Culture*. Douglas describes how American religion was "feminized" in the nineteenth century as the interests of women and evangelical clergymen became closely identified, and indicates signs of the "domestication" of parish churches. By mid-century, for instance, the church parlor became the center of congregational life. Increasingly standard church practices included church socials, flowers in the nave, the funeral "parlor," cemeteries that became landscaped "beautiful dormitories," the practice of embalming, poetic hymns extolling heavenly delights, sweet Jesus and God's abiding love. Episcopalian women were among the leading literary proponents of the sentimentalized church, notably the educator Catharine Beecher, the popular author Harriet Beecher Stowe who wrote *Uncle Tom's Cabin,* and Sarah Josepha Hale, the author of "Mary Had a Little Lamb" and long-time editor of *Godey's Lady's Magazine.* I could go on and on citing known and lesser known women who were leading "lights" in American religion and in local congregations. One daughter later summed it up with this impression: "Because Mother was so closely related to everything about . . . [the] Church, I thought, as a child, that the Church was an extension of our house."

Americans were drawn to religious enthusiasm by the successive waves of revivals that swept across the land from east to west. Most of the women who swelled the rolls of American churches by mid-century were converted, affirmed, or strengthened in their faith by the preaching of wandering evangelists. Nineteenth-century revivalism was a vast domestic missionary movement which started in one area and spread like fire to its neighbors. As I have said, the vast majority of citizens were unchurched at the start of the century and there was ample territory for evangelism. Central New York hosted so many evangelists that it was popularly dubbed the "Burned-Over District." Much of New Jersey and Ohio were similarly traversed. Revivals were the essential lifelines of American churches, supporting but not replacing parish life. Among those who had converted previously, revivals became occasions for deepening personal commitment, guarding against the "dreaded sin of backsliding," and learning new ways to share their convictions. Two-thirds of those who joined churches in the Second Great

Awakening (1790-1830) were women. Charles Grandison Finney, the leading pan-Protestant evangelist of revivals from the 1830s onward, publicly welcomed women's powerful talents. In his lectures "How to Create a Revival," Finney described women not only as objects of evangelization but as their very agents and promoters. Diaries kept by introspective Yankee women and newspaper accounts of tent meetings, popular occasions for conversion held usually in Southern states among both blacks and whites, depict women as dedicated revivalists.

Mothers were often the first to experience conversion; they then labored for their children's and husbands' souls. It is no wonder that a Brooklyn preacher in 1858 stressed the compassion of God "[who] pardons like a mother, who kisses . . . offence into everlasting forgetfulness." Converted women would then join others in regular meetings to pray for the conversion of their local community. A teenager from a small New Jersey town confessed somewhat guiltily to her diary that she spent "several delightful hours" in female prayer meetings. These gatherings were sexually-segregated groups of neighbors meeting weekly in good times for Bible study, and praying in bad times for the gift of another revival. We cannot underestimate the continuing drama, the rapture, the "flood of light and joy," as young people and women of all ages labored to exercise their talents as evangelists in their own homes and hometowns.

It is a mistake to think that America's evangelical activism was an extra-curricular activity that left mainline denominations unscathed. Evangelicalism has been, and continues to be, a dominant aspect of American religion. The Episcopal Church actively participated in the urban revivals of 1857 and 1858. Successive awakenings stirred this and other denominations to place increasing importance on personal conversion, to champion adult education, to move pulpits into the center of chancels, and to increase congregational singing. Albeit two of the most popular hymns, "Just as I Am" and "Nearer my God to Thee", were not allowed into the Episcopal Church's hymnal until 1874. I remember my maternal grandmother calling it "stuffy" and pulling out the Methodist version for family hymn-sings.

The most characteristic desire after conversion was to spread the Good News not only for the regeneration of souls, but also for the regeneration of society. For conversion was neither a private nor a personal event. In fact charismatic preachers and evangelical women were, in today's perspectives, radical "social activists." Their calls for conversion were thoroughly mixed with pleas for humanitarian reforms. Organizations for social reform were the direct offspring of evangelical revivals. Unlike today, the social agenda of evangelical Christianity was more apt to be improvement, not defense, of the status quo. Our ancestors would have been confused by a dichotomy between personal spirituality and social activism, or the belief that "a woman's place" was restricted to the home. Early in the century the abolitionist and defender of women's rights, Sarah M. Grimke, insisted that "the woman who prays in sincerity for the regeneration of this guilty world, will accompany her prayers by her labors." As another woman testified, "I must be up and doing!"

For many Christians, reform became their religion. Reform was a faith statement, not a cause. There were several spheres that attracted their efforts and energies. This era was characterized not by "single-issue" politics but by multiple reform activities commanding countless hours of service. Typically, activity for women began at home with the forming of maternal associations which combined hygiene and piety. Women urged one another to look first to their own "little family circle" for the means of producing

moral and social transformation. Soon other "fields of usefulness" opened up for their participation and leadership.
Abolition was at the center of reform movements. Women's
rights were another favorite emphasis of evangelical women,
most of whom would have supported the concept of today's
Equal Rights Amendment. Sarah Grimke's sister and companion in social reform, Angelina, envisioned the coherence
of religion, politics and reform as the very essence of Christianity. She wrote,

> [Moral reformations] are bound together in a circle
> like the sciences; they blend with each other like the
> colors of a rainbow; they are parts only of our
> glorious whole and that whole is Christianity, pure,
> *practical*, Christianity.

Our ancestors did not think about having to choose between being "political" or being "religious"; in fact they
would have been horrified by the theological and practical
implications of such a choice.

After the Civil War reform energies shifted from
humanitarian efforts on behalf of individuals to addressing
systemic social injustices. New organizations were founded
to advance women's suffrage, temperance and rights for
freed Blacks. Later in the century a remarkable woman
named Jane Addams pioneered the Settlement House movement to relieve massive social dislocation precipitated by
rapid industrialization and escalating immigration.
Relationships between social classes were the subject of
scrutiny. The new field of sociology would eventually catch
up with the wisdom of Jane Addams' assertion that "Hull
House was soberly opened on the theory that the dependence of classes on each other is reciprocal." Her most successful book, *Twenty Years at Hull House* (written in 1910 and still
in print) portrays her deep religious convictions and per-
suasive ability to raise up—in the midst of Chicago's impoverished Nineteenth Ward—a network of skilled

volunteer and paid workers. I still recall, as a young theological student about to undergo urban training in a Chicago ghetto, reading Addams's perceptive 1898 article, "Ethical Survivals in Municipal Corruption."

At the century's end, Susan B. Anthony insisted that "work is worship!" In terms of social reform movements in America, clergy did not lead the way. As Mary Sudman Donovan remarks in *A Different Call*, clerical enthusiasm for the new Social Gospel theology of the early twentieth century was a surprisingly "late bloomer," given the subsequent and substantial achievements by lay women reformers.

As in the sixteenth century, religious education nourished the ground for reform. Women and men who consecrated their lives to usefulness were cultivated in America's most influential institution for Christians of all ages, the Sunday school. This American lay institution was held in such high esteem that in 1910 Congress adjourned to watch the parade of the Adult Bible Class Federation. Sunday schools were pan-Protestant foundations, supported by what we would now call ecumenical organizations. They were designed to be "nurseries of Christians" and schools of faith for adults. As in the Reformation they encouraged basic literacy skills and the establishment of public schools. Schools also provided new occupations for women. Translating women's energies from working in the nursery to childhood schools was socially acceptable; besides, as one (male) administrator noted, women have been shown to be the "cheapest guardians." Volunteer workers were sent to teach "colored children" before the Civil War and "freed Blacks" thereafter. Schools were founded for American Indians, young girls in the West, and immigrant mothers in crowded cities.

It was a short step from welcoming women as schoolmarms to founding women's colleges. Here again religious motivation was primary. Mary Lyon established Mt.

Holyoke in 1837 for the education of women teachers and missionaries. The catalogue announced that "this new experiment" would make each woman "a handmaid to the Gospel and an efficient auxiliary in the great task of renovating the world." Lyon was an early instigator of another innovation in American education: discussion groups formed for the exchange of ideas.

Revivalism, reform and education, all coalesced to support the nineteenth-century passion for mission. Mrs. Franklin Fisk, president of the Women's Congress of Mission, reported to the 1893 Columbian Exposition (popularly known as the Chicago World's Fair) that "the spirit of missions is not simply a phase of Christianity, it *is* Christianity!" The Episcopal Church, like other mainline denominations, put "mission" into its official name, "the Domestic and Foreign Missionary Society" (1821). In 1850 other enthusiasts organized the Episcopal Missionary Society for the West— west, that is, of the Mississippi. Women organized for mission, first with inclusive Protestant female missionary societies and later in national denominational associations. The Women's Auxiliary to the Board of Missions (established in 1872) provided financial, psychological and other practical support to missionaries at home and abroad. The five standard fields for missionary "usefulness" were defined as foreign, domestic, diocesan, Indian, and colored. By the 1880s almost half of all Protestant missionaries were women. Toward the end of the century another lay initiative advanced the spirit of mission. Young persons joined together in the international World Student Christian Federation (1896). This autonomous student movement encouraged pioneering engagements in interdenominational and global mission. By the start of the twentieth century most Christians, their denominations and their parishes, were in a high missionary fervor.

The usefulness of Christianity thrived on the willingness of the laity to commit themselves to mission. Our nineteenth-century forebears expressed their religious lives largely in addition to worship on Sunday. They built uniquely American congregations with widespread lay control and participation. There were additional benefits in all this activity. Increasingly, as one preacher bluntly stated, "[we] talked to ladies as if they had brains." Women acquired new skills, solidarity, and friendship in well-organized reform movements. From their efforts we have inherited a practical, pro-education, and activist tradition, as well as institutions and occupations for social service and reform.

However successful these efforts were, there is still one serious cautionary note that must be raised about nineteenth-century American Protestantism and its missionary ethic. Reformers were not always welcomed or appreciated, nor were they tolerant of those who were different. The Protestant version of America's national destiny had overtones of imperialism and racism. These failings are underscored in Owanah Anderson's recent history of the Episcopal Church and American Indians, *Jamestown Commitment*. Values of class, race, and ethnicity were often narrowly conceived. This is another face of the expansion of American religion and the explosion of lay activity. Although there were occasional appeals for greater pluralism, the favored alliance of piety and politics in nineteenth-century America was distinctly Protestant. Cultural pluralism, for example cooperation with Catholics or Jews, was rarely expressed in action. By the century's end American laity were active and engaged in mission. Within this pan-Protestant, activist temperament, religious loyalties repeatedly clashed with the ideal of openness to others, a legacy that remained for future generations.

"The Real Battles of the Faith"

I was born soon after Pearl Harbor. I dimly remember overhearing my parents' whispered conversations about "the bomb" and their silence when we children later asked about Hiroshima. For this and other reasons it is not easy for me to talk about recent history. I find thinking about contemporary history akin to alchemy. "Golden" interpretations are made out of the "coals" of holocausts and daily living. My vision of Reformation England is clearer, refined through time. I see the most recent past "through a glass darkly."

A few insights do emerge with clarity. I do know that from the perspective of the historian, this century—more than any other—has been characterized by race hatred and political and religious genocide. I know too that from the perspective of Christian laity, the decade following World War II was marked by intense interest in the renewal of lay movements. These two themes are related. The moral chaos engendered by two world wars compelled many people to question and reinterpret implications of their faith, particularly as they thought about peace and security. Two centers of activity developed to support Christian laity. One focused on the reorientation of Christian values among ordinary working laity through the provision of adult education. Another addressed the limits of denominationalism as an basis for action and resulted in new ecumenical organizations.

As in the prayer from the Belsen death camp which began this chapter, suffering can produce moments of *focused* meaning. Out of crises, whether local or global, individuals and institutions can redirect their priorities, redefine their concept of mission. After the American Civil War, reformers turned to address systemic, social evils. In the aftermath of the Second World War, and in particular the Holocaust, the

concept of Christian civilization in Europe die
illusions about churches looking to secular c
tenance. The war years had illustrated
European churches, most of which remaine
Germany, to have an impact on their membership beyona
Sunday religion. Simone Weil, that paradoxical French mystic who died in 1943 and was much engaged with the suffering of others, insisted that "morality in the abstract," which does not extend directly to one's neighbor, is evil.

There was a new realism, a rejection of idealism and easy solutions, a recognition once again that the worldly calling of Christians was costly, demanding and essential. Simone Weil, Evelyn Underhill, Dietrich Bonhoeffer, William Temple, T. S. Eliot, Dorothy Sayers and others writing during the Second World War prepared the way. For example, Underhill—a scholar, mystic, conductor of retreats and a pacifist—described the "wilderness" that confronted her generation "in very harsh and concrete forms." She wrote in 1940 to members of a local prayer group of tensions that sound very contemporary:

> Most of you are very busy and often too tired or
> anxious to clear the space which is needed for
> concentration on God's worship. Practical life press-
> es more and more hardly. Strain is increasing. We are
> all more and more conscious of the uncertainties of
> our time. Not everyone can face the results of an air
> raid with an unshaken belief in the goodness of the
> universe and the loving-kindness of God. Institu-
> tional religion too often seems stiff, disappointing,
> remote from actuality in contrast to the awful realities
> of evil, danger, suffering, and death among which we
> live.

Her advice about spiritual sustenance was that it is not for our own sakes, but for the "sake of the world." She emphasized fulfilling "this-world obligations" while adhering to God's "other-worldly love." Underhill's message stands for our times as well.

As theologians during the war urged realistic assessments of suffering and evil—Bonhoeffer's phrase was "the cost of discipleship"—Dorothy Sayers similarly challenged idealistic attitudes toward social reform. In *The Mind of the Maker* this scholar, prolific author and writer of detective fiction urged her contemporaries to embrace creative thinking about such issues as peace, security and unemployment. Peace, she wrote, was not a problem calling for reformers' "devices" such as the Woman's Peace Party, founded by Jane Addams and Carrie Chapman Catt, or the League of Nations. Peace and security were not "problems to be solved" but "work to be made." Even more than solidarity, Sayers argued that a renewed creativity was called for, an artistic (we would say "holistic") expression summoning humanity to reflect "the mind of our maker." In theological terms, the doctrines of creation, of humanity, and of God's presence among us—themes addressed in the following chapter—provided theological justification for the commitments of these wartime leaders.

It is not surprising, then, that after the Second World War Christian leaders resolved to convince churches of the central importance of adult education. In Germany, Holland, Switzerland and other European countries lay leaders looked for direct, pragmatic ways to reconstruct Christian values. adult education was their strategic response. They spoke often of the need to rediscover what it meant to be Christian in "everyday occupations." German academies and conferences, called *kirchentag* or "church days," brought people with diverse secular vocations together with church leaders to explore the relationship between the church and the world. As early as September 1945 the first lay academy opened at the German resort town of Bad Boll. It was designed to attract teachers, journalists and lawyers, the three professions believed to have been most corrupted during the Hitler era. The goal was mobilizing laity out of passive, spectator attitudes toward finding active ways to express discipleship in the world.

A few lay training centers were established between 1945 and 1955 in North America, often with courses led by European exponents of the lay education movement. Many American congregations, experiencing a postwar "baby boom," focused instead on Christian education for children and youth, although religious educators repeatedly insisted that parents needed education, too. In the Episcopal Church the Rev. John Heuss, who led the newly created (1946) Department of Christian Education, proceeded to convince the church of the priority status of education for engaging "redemptive activity" in the family, in the parish and in secular society. Effective education, as one brochure noted, was concerned "for the impact of the gospel on the community."

Another educational leader with more radical social views, Adelaide Teague Case, insisted that "education, when it becomes socially dangerous, is surely beginning to be socially useful." Case, an experienced religious educator, was the first woman of professorial rank to teach at an Episcopal seminary, the Episcopal Theological School from 1941 to 1948. She was known for pithy sayings like "Think, don't dogmatize!" and "Lead, don't drive!" Her vision combined progressive educational methods and Christian social ethics. A listing of her religious affiliations reveals a religious openness and radical social agenda that was not typical of nineteenth-century reformers. Her memberships included the Religious Education Association, the Episcopal Pacifist Fellowship, the American Jewish Congress, the Student Christian Movement, Riverside Colored Orphanage, and the

Church League for Industrial Democracy (later called the Episcopal League for Social Action). Case would have understood the vitality of today's Latin American liberation churches, which are nourished and strengthened by adult Christian education and practical attention to basic social agendas.

Frankly, North American congregations are only now catching up with this wider social agenda as well as with Europe's critical appreciation of adult religious education. Education for ministry courses, offered in many Episcopal congregations, follow a methodology pioneered in the 1940s that asks laypersons to reflect on their daily lives and work using traditional and contemporary resources. This shifting priority toward adult education was signaled in a 1983 Church of England report, *All Are Called*, which defines adult Christ commitment as *"informed* commitment. It is not a matter of being loyal sheep."

Another postwar strategy for reorienting Christian churches and mobilizing the laity was ecumenical organization. The war years had demonstrated the structural poverty of denominationalism and the urgency of pressing for openness to others. Ecumenical alliances grew out of concern for practical cooperation among missionaries, and the global and interreligious dialogues of the Student Christian Movement. While there was little enthusiasm for merging mainline denominations, it was widely agreed that national and international Christian solidarity was essential for global peace.

The ecumenical movement of the late 1940s and early 1950s was animated by lay agendas. The first assembly of the World Council of Churches (WCC) held in Amsterdam in 1948 heralded the strategic significance of laity in the world. Hendrik Kraemer, Europe's leading theological exponent of lay ministry, became the first director of the World

Council of Churches Ecumenical Institute in Switzerland. It was innovative in those days to talk about the laity doing theology. At the second (1954) World Council of Churches assembly the Department of the laity was inaugurated. In this country the National Council of Churches of Christ (NCCC) was founded in 1950 to encourage effective interdenominational cooperation and witness. These postwar revival organizations championed lay persons not simply as members of congregations, but as valued workers in both local and global communities. The point was, as Kraemer put it, to look at laity not as "objects" to be converted but as "subjects and agents" fighting "the real battles of the faith."

The enormous impetus of laity in the history of Christianity should not be obscured. Historically laity have brought essential gifts to Christian societies and institutions. They have been successful organizers, pushing the frontiers of Christian mission beyond the confines of parochialism and denominationalism. They have identified pragmatic needs for reform and social welfare, shaping institutions and occupations accordingly. Lay people have broadened our social understanding, expressing diversity as a fact of life, not a problem to be solved. They teach us that churches are impoverished and even imperiled when they ignore the ministries of women and youth. They champion the extension of literacy and education as a means of liberation, repeatedly expressing the essential unity of social reform, work and worship. Sarah and Angelina Grimke, Jane Addams, Simone Weil, Evelyn Underhill, Adelaide Teague Case, and countless others have embodied a longing for spiritual vitality *and* social justice. It is impossible for me to tell the history of Christianity without recalling the spontaneity, vitality and commitment of generations of ordinary Christians.

I saw this piece of graffiti on the walls of a New York subway station: "Nostalgia isn't what it used to be." Christianity is not fundamentally defective, yet its bearers are far from perfect. The Second World War demonstrated once again that the worldly calling of the people of God cannot be taken for granted. Writing from prison towards the end of the war, Dietrich Bonhoeffer spoke of Christ's vigilance and our response:

> I discovered later, and I'm still discovering right up to this moment, that it is only by living completely in this world that one learns to have faith . . . By this-worldliness, I mean living unreservedly in life's duties, problems, successes and failures, experiences and perplexities. In so doing, we throw ourselves completely into the arms of God, taking seriously not our own suffering but those of God in the world—watching with Christ in Gethsemane.

We need not only knowledge of our history as the people of God, but also theological wisdom and courage. This is a subject for the following chapter. Yet this fact remains. Amid the witness of our ancestors and among everyday saints, there are stories of growth, struggle, moral failings, and transformation which we need to remember. The prominence of Christian laity in the church's formative events from the Reformation to our own day is at once sobering and inspiring.

ALL CAN BE THEOLOGIANS

Knowing Who We Are

In 1926 the Anglican theologian Charles Gore wrote, "Only those who know from the ground up what they believe, and why they believe, are able to help those who seek them out." Yet it may be difficult for those of us who are late twentieth-century Christians to believe that knowing about theology can be powerful. Yet for centuries our Jewish and Christian ancestors, some of whose histories we remembered in the last chapter, have struggled to claim this power. They have fought for personal access to the Bible and other formative documents of the faith, labored in mission and reform movements to express God's will, and endeavored to pass this inheritance on to their children. Knowledge of theology has been a central, powerful resource, even a basis for optimism. Theology has not only shaped religious practices and institutions, but molded the dominant outlook of cultures and civilizations. So theology—which is a people's understanding of God, humanity and the world—is not a neutral or dull topic. It is a subject that raises both enthusiastic declarations of certainty and endless lists of questions. It is an endemic source of tension, misunderstanding, and confusion as well.

There is a story from our Hebrew ancestors which illustrates the tension built into theological life and practice. This story is about a synagogue that had a conflict, a very bitter conflict about the *Shema*. In the Jewish tradition, the *Shema* is that most sacred moment in the Hebrew liturgy when the congregation says, "Hear, O Israel, the Lord is One God and you shall love him with all your heart, mind and soul."

There was one group in the synagogue that said, "When we have the *Shema*, we should stand in respect and reverence." There was another group that said, "We should sit in the posture of learning, as a symbol that we are being taught." And these two groups continued to argue until one day the rabbi said, "Well, the only answer to this conflict is that we should go to Mr. Finkelstein, the oldest living member of the original congregation. He is in a convalescent home. Let's go and ask him what the practice was when they started this synagogue."

So the rabbi took three standers and three sitters and went to see Mr. Finkelstein. One of the standers said, "Now, Mr. Finkelstein, surely when they had the *Shema* in those early days of the synagogue, you stood. Can you remember? Tell us and help us out of this impasse."

Mr. Finkelstein said, "I can't remember."

Then a person representing the sitters said, "Surely when that great moment of instruction came, you sat down to hear the *Shema*, 'Hear O Israel.'"

Mr. Finkelstein said, "I can't remember."

Then the rabbi said, "Now, Mr. Finkelstein, you've got to put your mind to this question and tell us what it was like in those old, traditional days. Tell us what you remember. Members of our congregation are now fighting each other, tearing each other apart. The congregation is divided and no one speaks to anybody." "That," Mr. Finkelstein said, "I remember!"

Like Mr. Finkelstein, we tend to remember behaviors, not rationales. Have you ever taken friends to church with you and tried to explain why some people are standing, some are sitting, and some are kneeling? Or have you found yourself explaining to newcomers how and when to use the various service books? These are not easy tasks. Often we seem to know by unreflective habit *what* to do without knowing *why* we do it. We use certain books in our liturgies, we adopt various poses and gestures. When asked why we do this or that, we frequently respond that we are following "tradition." Some of us are surprised to discover that even congregations within the same denominational family behave differently. Do we expect there is only one correct way to worship? When we do inquire into the theological basis for a religious practice, we are apt to receive differing perspectives. There are no timeless answers that determine specific responses to each inquiry. Questions about the theological foundations of our faith and the ways we worship yield equally diverse explanations. Many congregations include both sitters and standers.

Diversity in congregational worship is to be expected. It is an ancient and abiding reality among and within congregations. What worries me about today's patterns of worship is theological amnesia. We the people of this twentieth century have little in common with the religiously articulated cultures of our biblical, Reformation, and American ancestors. Bits and pieces of information, "how to" courses on spirituality, random Lenten lectures and Bible study classes are poor substitutes for the ongoing theological conversations of those men and women who have shaped Anglican theology.

I believe that our ancestors would be scandalized if they knew how little we remember or how much we take for granted without curiosity, inquiry or understanding. In this post-Christian culture all of us, laity and clergy alike, need greater familiarity with foundational theological texts. One remedy for amnesia is hearing what people have said and are saying, learning from past witnesses and from our contemporaries. We all can benefit from immersion in rich theological discourse, inviting ancient voices to join us in modern conversations.

I believe this journey in human understanding is an ethical as well as theological imperative. Understanding itself is a moral act; with so much going on in our society and world, *what* we choose to notice reveals *who* we are. Christianity is fundamentally a way of life that rejects separation between "being" and "doing." In other words Christianity is not an abstract philosophy, it is a living religion. Who we are and what we do speak volumes about our theology, our understanding of God, humanity and the world. We mislead ourselves, as well as others, when we forget to pay attention to the theological foundations of our faith. For instance, when our biblical ancestors failed to recall God's mighty promise of deliverance from oppression, they nearly decided to stay in Egypt and succumb to permanent bondage. In this century when European Christians during the Second World War turned from or denied the essential Jewish foundations of Christianity, their "forgetting" implicitly permitted the atrocities of the Holocaust, joining the name of Christ to that of the Nazi State. Theological amnesia has been dangerous. It can be dangerous again.

Such forgetfulness also has daily practical and pastoral consequences. When we go unnourished by our faith, we may also lack the courage and supportive conviction that enable us to work, laugh and love. When we are unable to express in our own words the theological framework of our denomination, we may find that we are ill-equipped to invite others into our churches. Evangelism, sharing the gospel story, is an informative art. For those of us who may be introverted, reaching out to others can also be a courageous act. Knowledge of theology equips us to welcome others with integrity, to help those who may seek us out. Additionally it prepares us to seek and enjoy wider unity through ecumenical conversations.

I have always associated understanding, learning from books as well as from family, friends and colleagues, with being a Christian. This impression was sealed in my baptism which I literally do remember. My brother and I were eight years old when we were formally adopted as church members in a service of Holy Baptism. Our baptism had been delayed because we were born in wartime, when the family could not gather. On our baptismal day we each received a Bible, the Prayer Book and, my favorite gift, a Brownie camera. I immediately put the camera to use taking pictures of the assembled throng of relatives and friends. That evening I read the Prayer Book from cover to cover, but fell asleep half way through Genesis. Sacred books, pictures, family, friends and the fellowship of a Sunday in May: these memories return whenever I am part of a baptismal service, and repeat the promise to "continue in the Apostles' teaching and fellowship."

Knowing who we are theologically involves both a specific and a general sense of identity. Growing up as a twin, I struggled to claim my own distinct identity, and to test and stretch this understanding within a large family. Similarly Christian identity is always bifocal, challenging us to look up close and further abroad. I am an Anglican, a participant in a worldwide communion of Christians whose lineage is related to events that shaped the sixteenth-century Church of England.

I am also an Episcopalian, a member of an American denomination called the Episcopal Church. Yet I wonder, just what do these titles actually entitle me to say about who I am theologically? Who are we as members of a specific branch of Christendom? What richness, what particular gifts, do we to bring to the whole people of God? What distinct theological inheritances continue to shape today's denominational gatherings?

Religious identity is not only a denominational subject. There is a more expansive fellowship. I am a Christian, a continuing participant in God's world household of faiths. At the same time any of us proceed toward deeper understanding of our own denominational families, we must acknowledge that Christians are members of an extended family of churches. All of us, sisters and brothers from many denominations, share in the biblical inheritance of Jewish and early Christian traditions. It is this larger biblical identity that I highlighted in the first chapter, recalling the church in the biblical story as God's created, chosen, pursued, sent and trusted people on earth. Religious identity is a many-splendored thing. It is a layered, cumulative inheritance. All Christians are apostolic inheritors of the world renewed in the image of Christ Jesus. Many of us draw upon traditions, saints, architecture and other achievements from the first 1500 years of Western Catholic Christendom. As a member of the Anglican Communion, I and others are part of a Protestant family of churches reformed around a biblical center. As American Christians, we are bearers of religions that our colonial ancestors formed to thrive in a frontier of cultural pluralism. As late-twentieth century people we live in a global village that includes vast religious and cultural differences, as well as distinct influences of nationality, race, class, sex, and ethnicity. These pluralistic global and social contexts continue to shape particular and general theological identities.

There are new theological Reformations liberating Christians throughout world today, and these will be the subject of the following chapter. Here I want to remember and highlight traditional Anglican theology as it was shaped during the first Reformation. My intent is to instill a deeper awareness of the foundational temperament of this theology by exploring predominant Anglican approaches to the Bible, creation and humanity. I embark on this recollection of Anglicanism's historical theology out of a sense of loyalty to our Reformation ancestors and a desire for continuity with their achievements. I share their words to enrich our dialogues.

Yet I write, too, with a sense of respectful urgency. If we fail to remember what formative Anglican theologians prized most of all, if we forget special hallmarks of our own denomination, then our theology will be rootless, increasingly susceptible to mimicking only contemporary secular passions, tossed to and fro from one generation to another without regard for past wisdom or future challenges. Without theological grounding Anglicanism, which already bears responsibility for continuity with certain Roman Catholic and Protestant legacies, will become not a middle road but a muddled journey. These reflections are intended to encourage ongoing debate and enlivening theological responsibility. Inquiry into the distinctive characteristics of the Anglican Communion is a continuing responsibility, far too critical a journey to be contained by an "Inquirers' Class" for Episcopal newcomers. Services of Holy Baptism and Confirmation invite all participants to deeper understanding; so does the Sunday Eucharist. In truth most of us have more, not fewer, questions as we mature in the faith.

For readers who belong to other denominations, I ask your tolerance as I engage in this often neglected piece of Anglican family homework. I seek your forbearance for what may appear to be lapses into denominational pride. This is an inevitable consequence of naming unique and distinctive characteristics in a single denominational family. I invite you to test these theological hallmarks within the context of your own religious affirmations. I urge you to reflect on what it is that you prize most in your own community, church or synagogue. Ahead of us is the longer journey, the ethical imperative to seek wider religious loyalties and deeper global understanding. Yet we must start with ourselves.

Religious identity remains a controversial subject. In the Episcopal Church and the wider Anglican Communion there are "sitters," "standers," and those continually in search of new postures. No wonder Mr. Finkelstein remembered arguments and conflict! Every family has its ups and downs. Journeys in theological understanding touch and embrace the diversity of God's creation. Within the Anglican Communion we can expect joy, loss, mystery and ambiguity. We will inevitably encounter confusion, tensions, and dissention. We may also find clarity, remembrance and the renewal of ancient promises.

"All Can Be Theologians"

All Reformation religions took root in a period of rapid religious change, as well as deeply rooted social struggle. Theological characteristics of new and reformed churches were shaped not in an age of piety but in one of violence and conflict. The litany of complaints expressed by early Anglicans has a familiar ring. In the 1500s they experienced galloping and unheard of inflation. Their fears were aroused by the invention of gunpowder and frightening new armaments. There was widening disparity between landholders and the rest of society, almost half of whom were chronically under-(or un-)employed. The poor flocked to cities, overcrowded centers of famine, disease, and despair. Average life expectancy was 29 years. Alcohol was built into the fabric of life; the average consumption of beer in England per man, woman and child, was one pint a day. Not surprisingly, most sixteenth century critics bewailed the collapse of public morality. In this violent, anxious society the early Tudor prayer books appropriately invited intercessions for "all sorts and conditions" of humanity.

The religious landscape, not unlike that of society today, was troubled and unstable. Theological conflicts escalated throughout the century as young theologians challenged traditional assumptions. Scholars and common people alike were challenged to reexamine their assumptions about faithful living and dying. Ancient authorities were attacked; people wondered how truth could be discerned among so many competing authorities. Some found answers in the Bible, others in Roman Catholic papal orthodoxy, still others in texts by compelling new writers of their day, such as Luther and Calvin. No doubt many people were confused, others apathetic. The Reformation produced an astonishingly wide range of questions, responses, assertions, theologies, religious communities, lifestyles, local patterns of worship, religious bigotry and hatred. By the century's end, throughout the continent of Europe wars were even fought over religion.

In this insecure environment ordinary people—laity and clergy—repeatedly turned to religion for security. Throughout Western Europe the Protestant Reformation largely resulted in confessional churches. In these churches, the ancestors of many of today's mainline denominations, members were expected to adhere to a set of tightly drawn tenets of belief, often lengthy statements of doctrine. Membership was based on these confessions of faith. Social realities in this tumultuous century seemed more conducive to producing detailed theological principles and rigid uniformity, than moderation and flexibility.

In England, however, the Reformation did not result in a confessional church or a single definition of religious truth. The theological temperament of early Anglicanism was marked by broad-mindedness, optimism, renewed faith in humanity, and a reasoned approach to biblical authority. By the end of the sixteenth century scholars of considerable theological and liturgical ability—including Thomas Cranmer, and John Jewel, Richard Hooker—shaped great books and lasting liturgies with moderate and flexible principles that remain foundational for Anglicans today. Under their influence the Church of England provided a broad framework for religious life, partaking of both Catholic and Reformed traditions, blended with English predilections for pragmatism, royal authority, parliamentary involvement and local custom. From its inception this so-called "classical" Anglican theology admitted wide interpretation, anticipated further theological movement and transformation. No one "confession" summarized Anglicanism. Indeed at the end of the sixteenth century Richard Hooker, the greatest exponent of classical Anglican theology, wrote positively of a church that rejected infallibility and assumed the right, indeed the likelihood, of changing its mind:

> The Church has authority to establish that for an order at one time, which at another time it may abolish, and in both do well.

Thus flexibility was built into the heart of Anglican theology.

Another characteristic was peculiar to founding Anglican theologians. They looked for a few essential theological principles and shied away from either excessively defining or overly restricting doctrine. In this regard these theologians resembled their Queen, for Elizabeth I spoke of "not seeking windows into"—or publically examining—her subjects' souls. Unlike other European monarchs, Elizabeth refused to torture or condemn citizens for their doctrinal opinions. During her reign the English church accommodated, officially and unofficially, divergent viewpoints. In a similar spirit in this century the American bishop, Stephen Bayne, insisted in a 1967 doctrinal report occasioned by charges of heresy against another bishop, that Episcopalians are not "inexorably bound" to any previous formulation of church doctrine. A few years later, in 1981, the Doctrine Commission of the Church of England concluded that "doctrine should be authoritatively defined as little and seldom as possible." This stance toward doctrine and appreciation of flexibility suggest that it is un-Anglican, perhaps even anti-Anglican, to seek narrow or precise doctrinaire definitions of what constitutes faithful practice, whether on specific aspects of moral living or on determining one correct way to describe or name God in worship.

Early English theologians did from time to time work on drawing up specific theological articles. The Thirty-Nine Articles of Religion, now printed as an historical document in the back of the Book of Common Prayer, represents these efforts. Church membership, however, did not depend primarily upon adherence to these or other articles; it depended upon baptism. The new catechism found in the back of the Book of Common Prayer illumines this broad-minded theological temperament and central definition of church membership. It presents in An Outline of the Faith a summary "point of departure" for teachers and other learners. Retaining the question-and-answer format of traditional catechisms, it provides expansive images of the church and inclusive responses to questions about humanity, ministry, and sacraments. For example, the response to the question, "Who are the ministers of the Church?" clearly includes all baptized people: "The ministers of the Church are lay persons, bishops, priests, and deacons." The biblical sacrament of baptism, not ordination or any other distinct status, grounds membership and ministry for all Anglicans.

During the Reformation a generous, inclusive definition of membership grew out of the optimistic expectation that most church members would *want* to know basic biblical principles of the faith and would in time become theologically informed, whatever their particular occupation. Erasmus of Rotterdam, a Catholic Christian humanist and formative Reformation scholar, wrote in the introduction to his translation of the New Testament: "All can be Christian, all can be devout, and I shall boldly add—*all can be theologians.*"

This was not mere hyperbole. Inspired by Erasmus' piety and erudition, English reformers believed that theological understanding based on the Bible was an ordinary expectation of faithful living. This is expressed in the central theological principle of the Reformation: all people are "justified by faith." Lay persons are not justified, or saved, by the intervention of clergy, or even by their own good works. Faith informs our journeys. Our ancestors thought men and women had the right and the obligation to search Scripture for basic theological understanding, as well as to express this understanding in their lives. Leaders of the newly reformed English church believed education in the scriptures was essential for laity and clergy. The goal of these early reformers was an educated church in which all might be theologians. Anglican theology, then as now, invites and depends on theological discernment among baptized members.

Digesting Biblical Knowledge

This optimistic, perhaps idealistic, advocacy of theological understanding for all people of God depends upon a unique approach to Scripture. There is a chicken-or-egg question here: which came first, a desire among ordinary persons to search Scripture for themselves, or a decision that the biblical record required new, contemporary interpretation. Both were components of the reformers' zeal. Early Anglicans adhered to the dominant Reformation insistence that the Bible "contained all things necessary to salvation." On this point our Protestant ancestors agreed: the Bible was *the* primary authority in matters of faith. Therefore it had to be translated into English, printed and distributed so that it could be read and heard throughout local churches.

Unlike other reformers, however, Anglicans insisted that the act of discerning what was biblically authoritative depended upon hard, integrative work involving the exercise of human reason. They knew that reading, searching and studying the Bible invited local questions, reflected daily concerns, and drew upon individual and communal experience. They believed the authority of Scripture did not, and must not, exclude the voice of the people. New interpretations were not only possible, they were to be expected. Anglican theologians advocated an accessible, non-literalistic, reasoned appeal to the Bible. Today the American biblical theologian and educator, Verna Dozier, recalls this legacy when she exhorts Episcopalians to remember that for us, "the Bible is fundamental, not fundamentalistic." This appeal to reasoned scripture is one of the most distinctive characteristics of Anglican theology.

By "reason" early theologians did not mean speculative abstraction, mere scrutiny or rationality. Reason was not simply intellectual ability or what we might call "intelligence." Archbishop Thomas Cranmer spoke of reason as an overall common-sense approach to the faith that excluded superstition. Richard Hooker believed reason was a gift from God, enabling all people to comprehend revelation. He defined reason as involving the full exercise of human nature, head and heart, affections and will, imagination and logic, emotion and intellect. In their pre-Enlightenment definition of "reason" Anglican theologians described a holistic experience of engaging the text. Reason was not the same as rationalism. This is an important distinction. The Episcopal theologian Virginia Ramey Mollenkott, who for 35 years was a self-styled "fundamentalist insider," describes biblical fundamentalism as "almost 100 percent cognitive, a rationalism that seeks to control reality by assigning a Bible chapter and verse to answer every mystery and quiet every question." This is not what Anglicans mean as a reasoned approach to Scripture.

Much like today's critical biblical scholars, early Anglican theologians regarded interpretation as an essential ingredient in biblical understanding. Human reason, broadly defined, informed interpretation. The exercise of reason allowed members of the church to find different meaning in different texts and contexts. Hooker wrote, "Words must be taken according to the matter whereof they are uttered." The Bible was not literally or unmistakably the "words" of God. God's revelation to all people, as recorded in the Bible, was the product of authors, editors and communities, however divinely inspired. Even those biblical texts which seemed clear and obvious, Hooker warned, required interpretation; Scripture is not a sufficient guide to itself. By this he meant that biblical passages naturally reflected the culture and situation for which they were written:

> The several books of scripture having had each some several occasion and particular purpose which caused them to be written, the contents thereof are according to the exigency of that special end whereunto they are intended.

Hooker also encouraged interpretation of individual passages, even whole books, in the light of the entire biblical record. In other words, he resembled today's critical, biblical scholars in advocating a holistic, contextual, and theological study of Scripture.

Then as now, this non-literalistic approach to the Bible demanded careful and prayerful study. John Jewel, in his 1562 *Apology for the Church of England*, stressed the diligence required of clergy and laity in learning the Bible:

> We allure the people to read and to hear God's word . . . we lean unto knowledge . . . we reverence as it becometh us, the writings of the apostles and prophets.

This exacting legacy is summed up in a prayer which still reveals the singular character of Anglican biblical study. Thomas Cranmer wrote the following Collect for the Second Sunday of the Church Year:

> Blessed Lord, which has caused all Holy Scriptures to be written for our learning; Grant us that we may in such wise *hear them, read, mark, learn, and inwardly digest them*, that by patience and comfort of thy holy Word, we may embrace and ever hold fast to the blessed hope of everlasting life, which thou hast given us in our Savior Jesus Christ. [emph. added]

More is required, in other words, than showing up at church services, listening to biblical passages, reading bits and pieces from the Bible. More is involved than marking, memorizing or quoting various favorite texts as "proof" of this or that belief. Cranmer writes that "all Holy Scriptures...[are] written for our learning." The whole of the biblical story is to be "inwardly digested." Cranmer's phrase recalls Jeremiah's description of devouring God's word:

> Thy words were found, and I ate them
> and thy words became to me a joy
> and the delight of my heart. (Jer. 15:16)

Cranmer's collect calls us to savor the Bible, to find it a source of basic theological nourishment. In more contemporary terms, we might speak of "integrating" God's word into our lives. Whatever our terms of reference, Bible study for Anglicans requires discipline. Anglican approaches to Scripture are not for the lazy, nor for those in search of simplistic answers. Biblical passages often raise uncomfortable issues. There are several passages I, for one, would rather omit. It is not easy for most of us to incorporate biblical wisdom internally so that it is, as stated in the Prayer Book, "not only on our lips but in our lives." "Inwardly digesting" the Bible was for Cranmer nothing less than the path to salvation. In his preface to the first Book of Common Prayer (1549), Cranmer suggested that the Bible was the compelling agent of conversion:

> The people by daily hearing of Holy Scripture read in the Church should continually profit more and more in the knowledge of God and be more inflamed with the love of . . . true religion.

For our early English ancestors the process of hearing, learning and conversion was never an isolated, individualistic journey. A reasoned approach to Scripture involved collective consideration and discernment. The good sense of the community, the neighborhood, the whole congregation, scholars and common folk, all were invited to discern biblical wisdom. No one person, no one biblical text, could stand alone. Cranmer used the collective, plural voice in the Prayer Book. Biblical reasoning was not based on what just one person said, or even what another person preached. Throughout the aptly titled Books of *Common* Prayer, whether written in 1549 or 1979, Anglicans were and are urged to read and interpret Scripture in community. This reasoned approach to Scripture is necessarily communal. As in the early Pauline communities, God's word is shared to inform church members and in turn build up the whole people of God. Private study is fine, but like private prayer, it is related to a central commitment to communal deliberations and public worship.

Reading and interpreting the Bible in community is also advantageous because the intentions and desires of ordinary people, like those of our Tudor ancestors and biblical forebears, become a part of ongoing conversations. Thus reasoned Scripture allows us to discover the historical nature of scriptural writings, as well as to interpret the Bible reasonably from the point of view of our own society. This particular method of Bible study invites us to honor our ancestors as well as to examine our own needs and desires. We do not have to choose between ancient and modern knowledge, ordained or lay leaders, street wisdom or academic scholarship. Many different voices enrich biblical conversations.

A contemporary Episcopal Church poster depicting the head of Jesus bears the legend, "This man died to take away our sins, not our minds." When I saw this poster, I realized anew what was at stake. The unique and life-affirming character of Anglican theology honors human abilities and responsibilities as well as God's action. Among American Christians today a reasoned, collective, and compassionate approach to the Bible may be the exception rather than the rule. Best-selling "how-to" books encourage individualistic appropriations of piety and solitary spiritual journeys, while Christian books cite specific "answers" to live by. In many televised church assemblies and the conservative yet popular Christian press, appeals to human reason are often attacked under the label of "secular humanism." Cranmer and Hooker would have found these contemporary attitudes, especially a belief in the inerrancy of the Bible, at least as difficult as Anglicans do today. They had the experience of contending against citizens of Tudor England, later called

Puritans, who believed that the word of God was abundantly, usually literally, clear. Anglicans and Puritans also did not agree about the authority of the Bible, about human nature, or about the wonder of creation.

Classical Anglican theologians were the precursors of contemporary, critical scholars of the Bible. They affirmed, and other Anglicans have followed, a standard for theology that joins human reason with God's revelation in the Bible. Anglican scholarship continues to delight in new learning. We welcome the findings of modern biblical research as well as those of archeological digs. These and other investigations help us understand more fully the social contexts in which our biblical ancestors lived. Uncritical or literal understandings of the Bible may be tolerated among Anglicans today, but these approaches are not representative. Both biblical literalism and the practice of citing one text to prove a point without theological comprehension of the whole story of the people of God, are not, theologically speaking, the Anglican way.

In our own tumultuous times I believe we cannot afford to dismiss theological attributes which our ancestors, in the midst of their own confusion and despair, found so life-giving. In particular we should not underestimate the formative value they placed on reasoned Scripture, their desire to integrate biblical knowledge into daily living, their advocacy of contextual biblical interpretation, their insistence that no one authority has a corner on biblical knowledge, and their balanced understanding of authority in general. As Anglicans we are entitled to emphasize the centrality of the Bible in matters of faith as it is interpreted through the critical, collective wisdom of the community. This distinct biblical method, prized by many of our ancestors, is fundamental. It is the foundation for a liberating theology of the whole people of God.

Rejoicing in Creation

In yet another way foundational Anglican theology is out of step with traditional Protestant theology and contemporary, conservative Christianity. Anglican theology has traditionally stressed the goodness of creation. There are two interrelated aspects to this affirmation. Anglican theologians have pointed to the excellency of the whole created order, and they have reverenced the earth, not heaven above, as the primary sphere of God's continuing operation. Anglican theology does not apologize for the fact that it is firmly grounded in society, in life in this world. The Prayer Book conveys these optimistic themes in a eucharistic petition:

> Open, O Lord, the eyes of all people to behold thy hand in all thy works, that, rejoicing in thy whole creation, they may honor thee with their substance, and be faithful stewards of thy bounty.

Again and again the Prayer Book asks us to go back to the Genesis story of a God who created as an act of love. It is as if we are called to share God's evident delight with each day of creation, repeating the biblical refrain, "It was good . . . it was very good."

For Hooker and for later Anglican theologians nature was, along with the Bible, another source of divine revelation. Hooker often wrote of the personal, authoritative character of God's relation to the created order: "All things are therefore partakers of God, they are his offspring, his influence is in them." In a lyrical passage from the *Laws of Ecclesiastical Polity* he describes several sources of wisdom:

> Some things she [wisdom] openeth by the sacred books of Scripture; some things by the glorious works of nature: with some things she inspireth them from above by spiritual influence, in some things she

leadeth and traineth them only by worldly experience and hard practice.

Next to the primary biblical base of knowledge, nature
joined revelation in teaching God's goodness. Joseph Hall, a
seventeenth-century bishop and author of the popular devotional guide, *Arte of Divine Meditation* (1606), encouraged his
readers to contemplate the glories of nature as "God's Great
Book." His contemporary, the naturalist John Ray, expressed
his appreciation in *The Wisdom of God Manifested in the Works
of Creation*. These and other authors laid the foundations of
natural theology in Anglicanism. Poets and mystics who
were to join in this estimation of the "glorious works of nature" included Samuel Taylor Coleridge, T. S. Eliot, Evelyn
Underhill and Annie Dillard.

In my childhood Anglican hymnody offered the most lyrical, certainly the most consistent, liturgical reminders of the
goodness of creation. There is the refrain, now repeated in a
contemporary novel and television series:

> All things bright and beautiful,
> All creatures great and small,
> All things wise and wonderful,
> The Lord God made them all.

Other favored lyrics from my childhood include, "For the
beauty of the earth,/ For the beauty of the skies,/ For the love
which from our birth,/ Over and around us lies . . . ", as well
as that powerfully specific hymn to joy: "Field and forest,
vale and mountain,/ Blooming meadow, flashing sea,/
Chanting bird and flowing fountain,/ Call us to rejoice in
thee."

This theological regard for the whole of creation goes
against the grain of most Protestant and Catholic thought.
There has been a dominant tendency in western Christian
theology to elevate human culture over and against the

natural world, to assume the one is civilized and the other primitive and chaotic. There has also been, at least since the Reformation, a hardening of mental or conceptual divisions between the so-called moral order and natural order. Max Weber, the eminent sociologist of religion, referred to this prevailing theme in Protestantism as "disenchantment with the world." The result of this line of thought has been not only the denigration of nature, but also an attempt on the part of theology to impose conceptual order on the external world. Yet Anglican theologians have rejected these suppositions, pointing instead to the essential goodness, and even the moral teaching value, of creation. For Hooker and his successors creation theology was and is formative. William Temple in *Nature, Man and God* declared that Christianity was inherently "the most avowedly materialistic of all the great religions."

In yet another way this Anglican emphasis on the goodness of creation is uncharacteristic of Protestant spirituality. Theologians from Thomas Cranmer to William Temple have reiterated the theme that the world is properly the church's work place. In his lectures on the Lord's Prayer Temple wrote, "Not *there* but *here* is the sphere of our spiritual concern; not *then* but *now* is salvation to be won and made manifest." Cranmer would have concurred. The informing vision of the English Reformation was a Christian commonwealth, a body politic that in its several interdependent parts yearned to recreate a godly kingdom on earth. Tudor idealism and the Pauline vision of the Body of Christ at work in the world permeated the Prayer Book and turned the attention of early Anglicans toward, not away from, their society.

In the terminology of political science Anglican theology has advocated a "one-kingdom" perspective in which church and society, although not identical, cohere and complement one another in cultivating God's reign on earth. The contrary view, represented in Puritan and sectarian Protestantism, advocated radical separation of spiritual life from secular realities. According to this perspective, the earth at best offered those who were among the elected saints a painful "pilgrim's progress" until they could partake of God's heavenly kingdom. As Hooker pointed out, the Puritans seemed to argue for two distinct and separate spheres for divine activity, while Anglicans have tended to emphasize the coherence of God's will throughout nature and history. Intercessory eucharistic prayers from Tudor prayer books begin with this instruction, "Let us pray for the whole state of Christ's Church militant here in earth." A contemporary version from the Book of Common Prayer bids us pray for "Christ's Church and the world." The social framework remains one of coherence, rather than a dualistic separation of the church from the world.

Grounding the work of the church literally in this world shaped the social and ethical framework of Anglican theology. One offspring of the Creator's direct engagement with the created order is the expectation that men and women will take up ongoing responsibility for creation. God is not indifferent to this earth or to the ways in which we inhabit it. Church historian John Booty has written that Anglicans are "environmentalists" in the truest sense, valuing as stewards the whole of the created order. Canadian and Native American theologians emphasize the fact that God created all things to live in balance, and our duty is to respect and sustain the resources of our earthly home. Edward T. Scott, until 1986 the Primate of the Anglican Church of Canada, recently reminded an audience that human accountability to God *in* nature, not *over* nature, includes the biblical command to replenish the created order, "to fill the earth" as well as to take dominion over it. (see Gen. 1: 26 and 9: 7) Bishop Scott spoke of the environmental imperative for righteousness, which he renamed "right-use-ness" of time, energy, and all other physical and natural resources. I am reminded, too, of a line from Francis Thompson's "Mistress of Vision": "All things . . . linked are,/ That thou canst not stir a flower without troubling a star."

Anglican regard for creation grounds us in this world. In this respect Anglicans resemble both and anticipate the worldliness of contemporary liberation theologians. Dorothee Soelle, for example, has made a direct connection between a positive theology of creation and the human longing for peace and justice. Soelle envisions human beings as co-creators, empowered by God for continuing the work of creation through our work and through our love. Implicit in this theology of mutual relationship is the assumption that God needs us to carry out our work in the world. Virginia Ramey Mollenkott also writes of a creation-centered spirituality whereby we turn to God for life, energy and meaning, while God calls upon us for embodiment and service. This responsibility is explicit in the peoples' post-communion petition from the Book of Common Prayer: "Send us now into the world in peace, and grant us strength and courage to love and serve you with gladness and singleness of heart."

Changing Lives

There once was an ancient and faithful Jew who lived between two bits of paper, one in each of his pockets. When he was full of enthusiasm for his own success and triumph, he drew the bit of paper from his right hand pocket and read: "You are dust and ashes." When he was despondent, crushed by the weight of his days, he drew the bit of paper from his left hand pocket and read: "For you, the world was created." To this story, Hooker and many other Anglican theologians might well have added, "But in your dust is the breath of God."

This story introduces a third hallmark of classical Anglican theology: a distinct regard for human life. This belief contradicts images and impressions that have dominated Christian thought, for Christians have not always believed that embodied human beings are important and good. A traditional and false dualism, inherited from centuries of medieval Catholic theology, wrenches flesh from spirit, body from soul, and gives the pervasive impression that only spiritual, unenfleshed humanity is of value to God. A hierarchical tendency in Protestant theology, moreover, elevates a so-called "high doctrine" of God over and against the vision of lowly, dependent human beings. This "God up there/sinner down here" framework projects doomsday images and a deep-seated pessimism about humanity. Turn on the televangelist preachers and you will find many who have forgotten that the biblical vision of the apocalypse was not given to ensure human helplessness, but rather to instill the refusal to surrender. In seeking to elevate God, this miscast theology of humanity inevitably denies the potential of Christian witness. It can victimize persons, instilling internal messages of self-hatred and worthlessness. Its external results can be despair and apathy, the fatalistic belief that we no longer make a difference in this world. This is not a base for building a theology of the whole people of God.

Classical Anglican theologians shaped an empowered theology of men and women from the Bible, the Prayer Book, and Catholic sacramental tradition. Yet instead of diminishing God, they emphasized the transcendent God of the Hebrews, the good giver of creation, who is addressed at the beginning of the Prayer Book service for Ash Wednesday: "You hate nothing you have made." This theme is underscored in the very first article of the contemporary Outline of the Faith, which defines human nature as "part of God's creation, made in the image of God . . . . free to make choices: to love, to create, to reason, and to live in harmony with creation and with God." The Prayer Book does not herald the unaided potential of humanity, but instead expresses confidence in God's good intentions, God's power and mercy. The American theologian Marianne Micks in her most recent book, *Our Search for Identity: Humanity in the Image of God*, argues that an anthropology that works at bringing humanity into focus has the central benefit of reaffirming God's presence. Indeed, Anglican assumptions about humanity inevitably lead us not to narcissistic introspection but to speak of God.

Anglican optimism about humanity depends on God's abiding grace. Cranmer emphasized that human efforts alone were not enough to win salvation. He spoke of the grace we are given to amend our lives as the foundation of human salvation. God's grace enables responsible belonging to God, rather than helpless submission under God. This hope is represented in the Prayer Book post-communion offering, appropriately called the People's Oblation: "And here we offer and present unto thee, O God, ourselves, our souls and bodies to be a reasonable, holy and living sacrifice unto thee." The direct implication is that God asks for the most important gift we have to offer, ourselves.

These assumptions about humanity are based on a theology of creation. They are even more explicit in the one doctrine which has been the guiding principle for Anglican belief and practice, the Incarnation. In New Testament theology the potential goodness of humanity depends on the Incarnation, that is upon the God who came to live among us both as God and as human. The Gospel of John proclaims this fully embodied doctrine: "The Word became flesh and dwelt among us, full of grace and truth" (John 1:14). The Incarnation also lies at the heart of Hooker's understanding of a sacramental church. He believed that God's purpose in taking on human nature was to change it, to better it and bring it toward conformity with divine nature: "God hath deified our nature, though not by turning it into himself, yet by making it his own inseparable habitation." For Hooker the Incarnation provided, through participation in the Eucharist, the basis for repeatedly binding men and women to God. Anglicans now express this incarnational relationship in the eucharistic petition that Christ "may dwell in us and we in him ."

There is yet another distinctive aspect in Anglican interpretations of the Incarnation, one that is seldom, if at all, affirmed by today's conservative Protestants. For many Anglican theologians the Incarnation has represented a radical exercise of mutuality that was for God's sake as well as our own. During the late sixteenth century, in a passage that is even more radical than Dorothee Soelle's contemporary description of human beings as "God's hands," Hooker writes, "We cannot now conceive how God should without man [humanity] either exercise divine power or receive the glory of divine praise." Michael Ramsey, Archbishop of Canterbury from 1961 to 1974, concluded that "the Incarnation meant not only that God took human flesh, but that human nature was raised up to share into the life of God." Ramsey traced the influence of the Incarnation in Anglicanism to nineteenth-century theologians Charles Gore, Henry Scott Holland, F. D. Maurice, and J. R. Illingworth, who in the formative *Lux Mundi* (1889) essays added that "it is impossible to read history without feeling how profoundly the religion of the Incarnation has been a religion of humanity." What does this mean practically? It means that we share responsibility with God in Christ for life in this world.

This also means that Anglican theologians have had to address the reality of individual and social sin. Our ancestors were not blind to human failings. They spoke of the waywardness, the selfishness of humanity. They were aware of the perversity of human nature. They realized that despite God-given talents, men and women sinned knowingly. That is why Tudor prayer books prescribed lengthy prayers of self-examination and preparation before participation in the Eucharist. Penitence and conversion is the process through which we repeatedly ask to be emptied of sins and filled with virtue.

Therefore Anglican interpretations of the incarnation necessarily include the Atonement. This essential theological relationship was underscored by Anglican theologian William Wolf in *No Cross, No Crown*. The atoning sacrifice of Jesus's suffering and death completes the assurance to all humanity embodied in the incarnation. An Outline of the Faith describes the Atonement as "[Jesus's] offering which we could not make; in him we are freed from the power of sin and reconciled unto God." Together the Incarnation and the Atonement express the saving, liberating character of Christianity; together they conclude that Christ has already acted for us. Richard Hooker described the movement of this relationship as "an alternation from death to life." He spoke of *metanoia*, a term used in the synoptic gospels for conversion from sin to God; it literally means a turning of the heart. For Hooker the action of repentance was the real transmutation. He wrote that the central intent of the Eucharist was to change lives, not bread and wine. Conversion as originally conveyed in the Prayer Book was for social amelioration, not privatistic or even personal gain. True conversion was socially redemptive, of benefit to our neighbors as well as ourselves.

Anglican theologians have long esteemed the lessons learned from human experience and from social relationships, but this is not an entirely new thought. The biblical record is grounded in the flesh-bound testimonies of witnesses. Biblical testimonies reveal that God is active in human history, whether the outcome is tragic, promising or ambiguous. Anglicans value human experience as continuing to reflect and respond to God's revelation. Hooker included "worldly experience and hard practice" in his listing of divine sources for wisdom. Experience, an essential component in shaping tradition, was also a necessary corrective against the corrupting course of time which, as Cranmer indicated in his preface to the first Prayer Book, had even marred worship. The point here is that Anglican theologians have valued not only human nature, but also human experience. William Temple insisted that we dare not ignore insights gained daily from our experience. As Archbishop of Canterbury during the Second World War he pointed to truth gained from the practical, economic and political strivings of humanity, from struggle in the midst of war as well as in peace. Like Hooker, Temple urged Christians to pay attention to world experience and hard practice, and to do so not by giving in to pessimism but by believing in the potential goodness of humanity. Those three distinct theological attributes—interpreting the Bible reasonably in community, grounding the church in the created order as the sphere of God's continuing operation, and affirming the salvation of humanity by grace—shaped the initial framework of Anglican theology. Together they convey the spirit and identity of Anglicans within Christianity. They also express a distinct theological methodology, revealing *how* Anglicans learn from Scripture, reason, tradition and experience. Anglican theology continues to be formed and reformed, amid conflict and tension, in accord with these several sources of authority. In 1965 Henry McAdoo, an English bishop, described the overall spirit or temperament that has been indigenous to Anglicanism since the Reformation:

> No human experience or field of enquiry can be alien to an outlook in which concern with the creation and the incarnation are to the fore. It will hold that theology owes to [the people] a rational consideration of their problems, and its method will be one of liberality. . . . preserving its ability to criticize as well as to interpret.

This discussion of classical Anglican theology has rested implicitly on two interrelated characteristics: the ability to live amid tension and conflict, and an overall tone of optimism about creation and humanity. Living with the tension and essential ambiguity of life is a different moral stance than striving to seek a middle course. The *via media*, or middle road, model for Anglicanism is misleading if it implies compromise solely for the sake of avoiding difference or tension. I prefer to envision Anglican men and women as on the road, *in via*, members of a church that endeavors to stay true to the biblical legacy of the mighty acts of God while undergoing movement, tension and change. Our theological and historical heritage suggests Anglicans have not solved tensions, but have struggled to live creatively amid conflict. John Booty writes that Episcopalians

> need not hide differences and keep peace so much as accept creative tension, assure constant dialogue, and anticipate gain from whatever conflict occurs within the orbit of mutual respect and love.

The anticipation of gain in the presence of conflict and mutual respect is an apt theological stance for a church that was founded at a time of extraordinary social unrest and religious change. This is also a realistic ethic for a worldwide communion that today harbors sitters, standers and those in search of new postures.

The biblical and social idealism of early English reformers continues today in the hopeful yet realistic contributions from more modern Anglican theologians: F. D. Maurice, Evelyn Underhill, William Temple, Marianne Micks, Desmond Tutu, Pauli Murray, Virginia Ramey Mollenkott, and many others. These authors offer collective encouragement not to escape from this world but rather to face directly into the diverse struggles and often harsh realities of life. Anglican moral optimism does not ask for blind faith or unthinking obedience, but for thoughtful and responsible commitment. While Anglicans emphasize the goodness of God's created order and the worth of human effort, they do not deny the fear of God or the reality of human sinfulness. These are abiding tensions within Anglican thought: fear of God and love of God coexist in our lives. According to the theological stance of the Prayer Book, however, it is love and not fear that inclines us to repentance. It might be said that Anglicans are theologically inclined to accept the "Good News" as truly good. Classical and modern Anglican theology provides a theological rationale for full participation by women and men. A conference of Asian Christians reported in 1973, "Lay men and women are . . . often the principal agents in discerning and responding to the Spirit of God." We are all invited to be theologians.

SEEKING WIDER LOYALTIES:
Today's Theologies of Liberation

Hearing and Knowing

> "It is no longer because of your words that we believe, for we have heard for ourselves, and we know that this is indeed the Savior of the world." (John 4: 42)

It has become almost axiomatic that if we are to believe anything, we have to hear it for ourselves. "Why, just the other day, I heard . . . . I know it's true, I heard it from Jane." We are accustomed to requiring first-hand witness accounts and to believing the testimonies of those we know, especially if we hear them for ourselves. I suppose this was often the case among our Christian ancestors. Ancient and modern believers, people like ourselves, tend to rely on first-witness accounts—whether they are Biblical testimonies or the confidences of our very best friends. Theology is for the living. It is grounded in human societies and relationships.

I believe it is important to emphasize this relational, collective nature of Christian life in the very beginning of a chapter on theology today. That is not just because I am a historian who usually focuses on the past. Many of us have a preference for past and future tenses, giving thanks for what

God has done for us and offering petitions to calm fears of what the future might bring. Yet we find it threatening to speak of faith in the here and now. We may be most threatened not by who we have been or by who we might become, but by who we actually are today. T. S. Eliot may have had this reluctance to live in the present in mind when he observed that "human kind cannot bear very much reality."

I suppose this is one reason why God had to send such mighty prophets, one after another, to command people's attention in the present. Israel's prophets were known to ask their contemporaries searching, probing, ultimately scathing questions. The prophets' words were usually addressed to groups of people, not isolated individuals, and their indictments were truth-telling depictions of their own times that spared no one. One part of the prophets' message was a call to respond to social evils that were imbedded in local social structures; Amos, for example, spoke out against the rich "who sold the needy for a pair of shoes." We too need to hear news from today's religious leaders that focus on our own culture, our own local structures. Like our biblical ancestors, we cannot afford to dismiss prophetic, social messages. Guilt and lethargy often result when an institution—whether it is the state, a church, a school, or even a family member—stresses individual accountability in isolation from social reality. Listening to prophetic voices, hearing and knowing what to believe, calls us to listen and respond together.

This chapter focuses on hearing and knowing about the most significant theological revolution in the life of churches throughout the world: today's theologies of liberation. I have chosen to speak of "theologies" in the plural for several reasons. First of all, theologies of liberation are not brand new. The themes of captivity, exile, wilderness, longing for freedom, welcoming salvation are intrinsic to our biblical identity. What we might call "yesterday's" theologies of liberation, each of them biblically based, included not only the Protestant and Catholic Reformations but also Evangelical, Methodist, utopian and other movements, some of which created today's churches. Second, we are currently witnessing the simultaneous genesis of several liberation theologies, each with a different social and/or geographical base. These include Latin American liberation theology, Black theologies of liberation, feminist liberation theologies, Asian, Chicano, Native American, and similar liberation movements. With their distinct particularities and common characteristics, liberation theologies and churches represent ways Christians today are developing fresh theological assumptions and articulating contemporary first-hand witness accounts.

Perhaps the last Copernican revolution in theology was occasioned by Luther's "new theology" of Wittenberg, proclaiming justification for all faithful believers and drawing texts from Pauline epistles that encouraged faithful living rather than pious works. The favored biblical theme of today's "new theologies" of liberation is the salvation of oppressed peoples. Liberation theologians speak of the need to work for salvation in this life, salvation that is born of people's struggles for freedom and well-being. In their affirmation of a gospel of earthly salvation, liberation theologians recall the Exodus story of God's intervention on behalf of the enslaved Israelites whom Moses led out of bondage in Egypt into the wilderness of the Promised Land. The significance of the poor in Israel's life as participants in their own salvation, and as God's own chosen people, is underscored by texts such as Isaiah 61:1 and Luke 7:22, passages that command us to continue the work of feeding the poor, sheltering the homeless, freeing the prisoners, caring for the broken-hearted, comforting those who mourn, and proclaiming God's favor to the afflicted. They point to the liberation of the poor as Jesus's central mission, the message he chose to read in the synagogue at Nazareth (Lk. 4: 16-20). Liberation theologians believe that Christians throughout the world today are still commanded to carry out this change, to work with and for the relief of oppressed people wherever they may be.

Much as Luther's new books of theology "made head-lines" in the printing presses of Reformation Europe, the theological texts and first-hand accounts of contemporary liberation theologians have, for the past twenty years at least, been making news. Take these newspaper reports occasioned by John Paul II's 1985 visit to South America. From the perspective of Gustavo Gutierrez, a Peruvian Indian priest and well-known liberation theologian, the Pope's visit *"was* theology. [Because] it was important that the Pope, a mythical person for the poor, actually talked about social injustice and their problems." A local Peruvian parish priest, commenting on the same visit, claimed his people found a renewed sense of their own honor through the papal visit. "They thought about it and said, Yes! We are the people of God!" Recently the *New Yorker* extensively profiled the tiny Brazilian slum of Campos Eliseos. Frei David, the liberation priest of this poor town who labors to heal the disease he calls "the violence of helplessness," reads Exodus and Luke for inspiration and ministers in what is called the People's Church. Frei David patiently explains that his and other liberation churches are enlivened by the "embracing concept" of liberty which has been missing until now:

> We have to remind ourselves that the real Church is with the community, that it strengthens as the liberty of the people—who distribute the Word of God—strengthens.

What do journalists' stories about the politics and poverty of a Latin American people suggest to us? What have liberation theologies to do with ordinary routines of Christian churches in North America? What if we honestly prefer theologies that comfort us rather than theologies that stretch us? What need have we for liberation, if we do not feel oppressed? The biggest question of all is, why should so-called North American Christians hear and know about liberation theologies? I think these are all open questions, inquiries to keep in front of us as we risk learning from Christians today who are continuing to respond to liberation themes.

At least one theologian, Jurgen Moltmann, has suggested that a successive pattern of freedom movements has characterized western society. I find it helpful to think of liberation theologies as collective reform movements that are revitalizing and deepening mission in the people's churches of our own day, much as the Reformation in sixteenth-century Europe gave birth to Protestant churches and revitalized Roman Catholic communities. We have much to learn from, and need not fear, the kind of liberating movements that resulted in the formation of Anglican and other churches. In other words, liberation theologies are the reformation movements of our own day.

There are clear distinctions of emphasis, need, and location. Liberation theologies are first of all about the people of God, the church as it is made up of people, not about institutional churches or about the "re-formation" of official religious doctrine. Basic survival, justice and peace issues—in other words, practical engagement with daily human needs—shape the theological agendas of liberation churches. Members of liberation communities address challenges faced by ordinary people: hunger, housing, poverty in all its guises, human rights, political rights, external and internal freedom from demeaning histories, righting oppressive imbalances in human relations, and liberation from the inexorable grasp of racism. Liberation theologies have also taken deepest root in those geographical areas of Latin America, Africa and Asia where the European Reformation was no more than a cultural agenda imposed on indigenous religious groups by missionaries and colonialists. Liberation theologies have appealed as well to those who were not instrumental in shaping the official progress of the European Reformation: women, people of color, and the poor. As we've noted earlier, the twentieth century is marked by genocide, that is, by the deliberate destruction of peoples for their religious, political, racial, and ethnic identities. Thus it is not surprising that new theologies in the last third of this century center on the liberation of such oppressed peoples. Perhaps we are now preparing for a new age, a new millennium, a time which continues the traditional Jewish and Christian legacy of yearning for wider liberation.

Liberation theologies raise challenges that, as in the days of Israel's prophets, stretch both our individual and collective capacities for hearing and knowing. Their theologians have much in common with Amos and Jeremiah. Their descriptions of the present are painful to hear, their indictments (whether we admit it or not) touch us, their challenges produce new life as well as occasional rejection. Take, for example, the writings of the contemporary Protestant ethicist Robert McAfee Brown. Brown is only one of several American theologians working to translate concerns raised by these theologians of the "Third World" into terms that directly address those of us enjoying the prosperity of the "First World." Brown does not mince words in asking where our first loyalties reside:

> If our first loyalty is to the United States, we will resist the notion that our nation is a predator; if our first loyalty is to our white skin, we will resist the notion that whites have been ripping off nonwhites; if our first loyalty is to our class, we will resist the notion that it is on the side of repression and destruction; if our first loyalty is to the institutional church, we will resist the notion that it is deeply complicit in the evil

deeds that darken our world today. All such loyalties are too parochial, too partial. They must be shattered, for they in turn are shattering human hopes everywhere. We need a wider loyalty . . . .

It is hard to know what to say after reading Brown's pointed challenge. We might comfort ourselves with the recognition that the traditional words of biblical messages are often uncomforting! To have our basic loyalties challenged seems to go with the territory of being Christian. We might dismiss Brown, along with other liberation theologians of the First and Third Worlds, as ideological heretics. That is a frequent, historical Christian response, dismissing what we do not want to hear as heresy. Or we might insist we are too busy, too old, or too preoccupied to learn new information. In adult education, I have observed that even the knowledge we bring to it can be a barrier to learning. One of my favorite sixteenth-century theologians, the Catholic reformer and wit Erasmus of Rotterdam, challenged adults of his generation through insisting that "by identifying the new learning with heresy, you make orthodoxy synonymous with ignorance." In other words, closed-mindedness breeds the wrong conclusions; those who search for theological wisdom must be open to both continuity and change. As in the sixteenth century, we need to address seriously challenges from today's "new learning."

We might also consider the social nature of challenge, wondering what theological gifts and skills we already possess that could help us hear and know what to believe. As a historian I know that serious social challenges differ from age to age, yet as a theologian I believe that how we encounter challenge is related to our fundamental corporate identity as Christians. We speak of the desire for healing our minds and bodies, of the need for compassion toward those who suffer, of the responsibility to strive for peace and justice, of respecting the dignity of every human being. When we consider these and other legacies of our faith, I believe we will recognize that we already possess continuing theological resources for hearing and knowing about liberation theologies.

Social and Personal Transformation

Anglicans actually have a head start on understanding liberation theologies' vision of social transformation. As I said in a previous chapter, our inherited theological perspectives on creation, humanity, and God's continuing presence in our daily lives have endowed us with a legacy that anticipates communal tension and change. An emphasis on social transformation has characterized Anglican worship ever since its earliest prayer books expressed the ideals of a social commonwealth, healed in part through particular and repeated intercessions for "all sorts and conditions" of humanity. Social transformation is a desired outcome of Christian life and Anglican theology, as we saw before.

In this century William Temple once again called the church to recover her true, civic and corporate identity in *Christianity and the Social Order*. In many respects Temple, writing in the midst of the Second World War, was summoning the church to a justice-seeking commission that is similar to today's liberation theologians:

> Why should some of God's children have full opportunity to develop their capacities in freely-chosen occupations, while others are confined to a stunted form of existence, enslaved to types of labour which represent no personal choice but the sole opportunity offered? The Christian cannot ignore a challenge in the name of justice.

Temple would also concur that this ecclesiological commission is not distinctly Anglican, but foundationally biblical. Its purpose is derived from the earliest and most frequent

biblical metaphors for the church, the Body of Cl
people of God.

These and other biblical metaphors recall ou
interdependence. They express a value as clear and ...ient
in respectability as the command to love our neighbors as
ourselves. One cannot function in isolation from others and
still be a Christian. Someone who is totally out of touch with
others is not a Christian; an "autistic Christian" is an
oxymoron, a contradiction in terms. One of the greatest
theologians of this century, H. Richard Niebuhr, once wrote
that "no self exists or knows itself save in the presence of
another self." This may be one reason why children invent
or adopt imaginary playmates. For instance I have a lifelong
fondness for that silly old bear, Winnie-the-Pooh:

> So wherever I am, there's always Pooh,
> There's always Pooh and Me.
> "What would I do?" I said to Pooh,
> "If it wasn't for you?" and Pooh said: "True,
> It isn't much fun for One, but Two
> Can stick together," says Pooh, says he.
> "That's how it is," says Pooh.

As children, we naturally look for playmates. As we grow
older, teenage social patterns remind me of our need to "hang
out" in groups. As adults we sometimes forget or forgo the
pleasure and the solidarity found in the company of others.
Groups can also inspire courage. The feminist liberation
theologian, Carter Heyward, tells the story of a Quaker
woman at a peace rally who spoke of two "solutions to our
feelings of powerlessness: 1) Do something. 2) Do it
together." Pooh would have agreed.

Individualism—in Webster's first definition, "leading
one's life in one's own way without regard for others"—is
counter-productive for Christians. Michael Ramsey claimed

that individualism has "no place in Christianity, and Christianity verily means its extinction." Ramsey pointed to liturgical renewal movements and the rediscovery of the essential communal nature of the sacraments of baptism and Eucharist as central to Christian identity of first importance to Anglicans. Still, as Christians we live with an inescapable tension; we honor human particularity and at the same time are called to seek wider universality. Each of us, as an individual, does matter to God. There is a particular aloneness to birth and death, and a resolute individuality to the private prayers we offer throughout our lives.

The American theologian Marianne Micks captures this paradox of our identity by describing human life as "both irreducibly social and irreducibly singular." By implication, then, none of us by ourselves has a living relationship with God. Even Julian of Norwich, the fourteenth century mystic who lived cut off from most of humanity in an anchorhold attached to the side of a medieval church, often wrote her visions or *Showings* of God in the plural voice: "Peace and love are always in us, living and working, but we are not always in peace and love." Julian of Norwich would no doubt have concurred with Marianne Micks' assertion that our transformation is a social response:

> No one is ever transformed in isolation from other human beings. Even a devout hermit in his cell on Mount Athos prays in the fellowship of the Body of Christ . . . Human liberation and human transformation are two names for the same phenomenon.

If this is true, then our transformation—seeking to set one another free in Christ—is an ancient and abiding social expectation.

Social transformation depends on more than our ability to remember that we are not alone. I believe its theological essence is conveyed in the gifts of divine and human compassion. Human compassion does not mean pitying others; literally it means "with passion," suffering and enduring with others. As he traveled to the cities and villages of Galilee, it was often reported of Jesus that when he saw a harassed crowd, he would "have compassion on them" (Matt. 9:36). Yet people assume that given the fact of the Holocaust and the threat of our nuclear arsenal, God has chosen to walk away from crowds, to abandon human history. Instead I think it is we who may have given up our belief in divine compassion by making images of God that are too small. Elie Wiesel, the premier novelist and Jewish theologian of the Holocaust, writes provocatively in *Night* of a God who suffers with us, a God who, whether we wish it or not, is part of the agony of this world, a God who can hang utterly helpless on a gallows.

Perhaps it is not God who is abandoning us, but we who are abandoning one another by no longer demanding compassionate judgments from each another. If we believe the biblical assertion that we are created in the image of God, saved by the One who had compassion on crowds, then we are also called to express compassion by bearing with one other's suffering in this world. It is worth repeating Bonhoeffer's advice to "throw ourselves completely into the arms of God, taking seriously not only our own sufferings but those of God in the world." In his final talk hours before his death, Thomas Merton spoke of compassion as "based on a *keen* awareness of the interdependence of all these living beings, which are all part of one another and all involved in one another." Compassion is itself a transforming awareness of our intimate relation with creation. This is one reason I find both mystics and poets such valuable Christian companions.

This vision of the interdependent nature of created life calls me to a greater awareness that sin as well as redemption has a social dimension. When I was a child I believed that sin had to do with breaking things, dropping a china figurine I'd been told not to touch, or going back on a promise to help my twin brother. The sin I knew best was lying, or, in the old language, "bearing false witness" by concocting stories that fit my own wishes. In my childish vision I saw sin as something done by one person, in isolation. Actually the new language for the ninth commandment in the Prayer Book catechism is more complete: we are instructed "to speak the truth, and not to mislead others by our silence." Sin in this and other definitions involves broken relationships; it is always social. During this century theologians have perceived sin as turning away from truth, denying reality (our own and others'), and constructing unreal worlds. In *The Symbolism of Evil*, Paul Ricoeur explains how "evil takes root at the point of the individual's disorientation from the larger reality." Some of its early signs and symptoms are treating others contemptuously, building a life only around one's self-interest, and denying ambiguity. Lionel Trilling, an American essayist, once wrote that the most destructive acts are committed by people who have no doubts. During graduate school, I was fortunate to study briefly with Paul Tillich and to hear him preach on several occasions. One of his repeated themes was North Americans' pathological anxiety, our preoccupation with security, certitude, and perfection. The Canadian psychologist and theologian James Wilkes summarizes Tillich's recognition of contemporary evil in these terms:

> The truth is [we] cannot have absolute security, certainty, or perfection. To want them is understandable, to demand them is diabolical, and to believe that one has already attained them is madness. Evil can readily be found in their pursuit.

Brokenness, distortion, rejection of the social realities of life itself shape our singular and social sinfulness.

Today's liberation theologians reveal and name—in order that they might be healed—categories of social sinfulness that separate us from one another. Liberation theologians employ terms often ending in "ism" to denote distortions of human life. "Racism" depends on the objectification of persons as inferior beings because of their skin color, ethnic or racial origins. Hitler's vision of a pure, white race was no anomaly, for people of darker skin colors—whether black, red, brown, yellow, and darker white—have historically been enslaved by lighter peoples. "Classism" pertains to power imbalances rooted in structures and attitudes that characterize people according to their economic standing, punishing some and rewarding others. "Sexism" denies full humanity to women and assigns rights, dominion, and the interpretation of truth to men. Feminist theologian Rosemary Ruether defines sexism as "broken mutuality between the genders." These and other "isms" bespeak moral degeneracy within our families, neighborhoods, churches, and the whole social fabric.

Liberation theologians point to "clericalism" as another distortion of life among Christians, one which we seldom address openly and persistently. "Clericalism" exaggerates the status of clergy while devaluing and patronizing laity. In this mutually disabling relationship, distinction among church people is turned instead into divisions between them. Such separations in function and status raise questions about how we can be different but not alienated, neither domineering nor passive, patronizing nor lazy. Symptoms of clericalism include intimidation, hoarding educational resources, controlling so-called "real" theological language, congregational passivity, and renunciation of authority. One clear example of clericalism is to describe a congregation which is searching for a new rector or vicar as "vacant." In clericalist language laity are often invisible, even in those moments when their energy is most in demand.

Yet clergy and laity both participate in clericalism. There are laity who expect clergy to be elitist and who sharply separate church from society; there are clergy who see part of their role as giving laity jobs to do in church, and whose own theology of authority places them somehow closer to God than to the people of God. Clericalism thrives on low expectations of lay people. Ultimately it inhibits the mission of the whole people of God. Liberation theologians reject clericalism and instead place great expectations of the collective authority of gathered, local communities. As one Salvadoran priest (who was later murdered for his advocacy of his people's liberation) insisted, "Brothers and sisters, God expects a great deal of you now."

Liberation theologians in Africa, Asia and Latin America also address the "ism" called "colonialism," a lethal combination of clericalism, racism, and economic exploitation which turns religion into a tool of the status quo. In "colonial" theology, missionaries save souls while secular elites profit from natural resources and minerals, taking control of land use and enslaving local peoples through economic or military means. Colonialism continues in today's pursuit of a global assembly lines, zones where economic exploitation proceeds without serious restraint. For example, in the state of Rio de Janeiro, "it is often said, twelve million people are starving, twelve thousand people are swimming, and anyone who is neither starving nor swimming is up to something terrible." Colonialism accommodates vast extremes in wealth and poverty, which in turn encourages obedience to the church and state despite the misery of the present. Theologically, poverty is accepted as God's will and wealth as a sign of God's blessing, as if exploitation of the poor did not matter.

In their delineations of racism, classism, sexism, clericalism, colonialism and other social expressions of oppression, today's liberation theologians join the witness of the Hebrew Scriptures and the New Testament in pointing beyond personal morality toward complicity in social sin, itself embodied in cultural and economic relationships. Rabbi Abraham Joshua Heschel has written, "Some are guilty, all are responsible." Can we avoid a sense of responsibility when we "mislead others by our silence"? We may try to excuse ourselves from wider responsibility by adopting either a privatist position—"It's none of my business"—or a neutral, "objective" position, as if we were likely to be morally correct when we are most detached and disengaged. Anglican Archbishop Desmond Tutu of South Africa is fond of saying that if an elephant is stepping on a mouse's tail, the mouse will not appreciate a bystander's neutrality; neutrality in a situation of injustice places us on the side of the oppressor. Still, you and I may wonder how North Americans acquiesce in the oppression of other peoples. The particular context and character of liberation theology in Latin American provides another vision of mission with which to test our own personal and social biases.

Voicing Local Theologies

T. S. Eliot once said that we are not well educated, or even knowledgeable about ourselves, unless we know the words, signs and symbols of a second language. Many of us experience increased self-knowledge when we travel abroad. Other cultures can serve as prisms, distant mirrors, through which we may see our most cherished values more clearly and even catch a glimpse of deeply held yet unexpressed assumptions. Temple, Tillich, Heyward, Tutu, Wiesel, Ruether, Brown and other twentieth-century theologians have repeatedly summoned North Americans to pay attention to the responses of other cultures to liberation themes. There is good news in today's liberation theologies: wisdom may be found in the faith of the poor. The possibilities ahead are signaled in the title of one of Robert McAfee Brown's newest books, *Unexpected News: Reading the Bible with Third World Eyes.*

I want to explore what is most creative and most unique in contemporary liberation theologies, particularly as expressed by members of Latin American liberation churches and their theologians. Their voices convey spontaneous enthusiasm, the power of evangelization, and the hope for social renewal that is at work in their churches. A local Catholic worker, Sister Maria Hartman, writes:

> What has happened to the Church in Latin America is extraordinary. I think about that when I go to the U. S. and see how the Church is there. I think you are so backward! And they never believe me. Because they think about the third world, and assume we are underdeveloped. But as far as the Church is concerned, my God, we are very developed.

According to Leonardo Boff, a candid and compassionate theologian of the liberation movement that calls itself the People's Church in Brazil,

> we are living in privileged times. There is an upsurge of life in the Church that is revitalizing the entire body from head to toe. The Church has been placed on the road to renewal, which will surely result in a new manifestation of the Church as institution. There are powerful and living forces, particularly at the grass roots.

They speak of churches "living in privileged times" and of churches that are "very developed." Their comments suggest that North Americans may have "underdeveloped" churches; perhaps we need to assess our definitions of mission, learning from those who are revitalizing local churches "from head to toe."

One of the essential observations about liberation theologies is that they are birthed by particular living communities. This is the first and most central common denominator: liberation theologies are always rooted in the concrete. Gustavo Gutierrez, whose 1971 *Theology of Liberation* was for many North Americans a first introduction to the accomplishments of Latin American liberation theology, insists that living theology begins not with the introduction or assertion of abstract doctrines, but within the daily struggle of living communities. For instance, Frei David's first step in the favela of Campos Eliseos was to turn the parish house garage into a trade shop for local boys, who were stealing because they had no jobs and no prospects of any. This local priest soon discovered that the boys were the best judge of community needs; building church pews was replaced by gates and other devices to make neighborhood shanties burglar-proof. For Gutierrez and other liberation theologians, the theology of the people's churches are shaped by the particular experience of a local community. The European Catholic ecclesiologist, Edward Schillebeeckx, concurs: "Practice [work and worship] must never wait for the permission of theologians before it gets going." The term they use for building theology from local custom and experience is "contextualization."

The learning mode, the pedagogy, of liberation communities was first suggested by Paolo Freire in *Pedagogy of the Oppressed*. Freire describes a process of mutual enrichment in which learners take responsibility for naming and claiming their identity, needs and strategies for action. It is a method of enrichment that has much to teach First World Christians in their own parishes and communities. He believes that a peasant literally discovers his voice and is transformed by speaking publicly in front of his friends. In the "schoolroom" of the community, all are teachers and all are learners. Within these small liberation churches each member is a working theologian, contributing to the construction of local theology as they address daily problems like lack of water, usury in the market place, alcohol and despair. The best known example is the fishing village of Solentiname, which participated in the development of a book of local theology later published by its pastor, the poet Ernesto Cardenal, as *The Gospel in Solentiname*. This way of learning for mutual and social empowerment, which is so much a part of local liberation communities, is called "conscientization."

These large words actually describe local practices. Throughout Latin America there are gathered churches called *comunidades eclesiales de base*, a name sometimes shortened to CEB's, or base communities. These communities are formed from the "base" of society, the poor, and the base of the church, the laity. Boff calls this movement "ecclesiogenesis," a new church born of the old from the darkest, poorest recesses of humanity. In these communities the Gospel and the local culture combine to produce what Boff depicts as "a Church being born from the faith of the poor." In a recent book, *Faith of a People: The Life of a Basic Christian Community in El Salvador*, the daily life and the formation of a poor church are described by the local priest Pablo Galdamez (a pseudonym). Galdamez recalls,

> Our communities started with people. People looking for salvation. Salvation that went by the name of happiness, friendship, love, justice, life, peace. A great number of people in El Salvador were looking for all this because they didn't have it.

Gradually, Galdamez realized, the people of this community came to believe in themselves. They overcame feelings of weakness and powerlessness to organize themselves not only with assignments to convene weekly catechism classes, Bible reading groups, and mission teams, but also as agents to plan squatters' strikes, meetings about land rights, and teams to work for the provision of water and electricity, better train schedules, and support for the market women. Frei David in Brazil insists that the poor of his base communities are political "only insofar as the issues that concern them— jobs, land, housing—are political." The recessional hymn from the "Salvadoran Mass of the People" describes the commitment of the poor to fight against oppression:

> When the poor seek out the poor,
> And we're all for organization,
> Then will come our liberation.
> When the poor proclaim to the poor
> The hope that Jesus gave us,
> That's the Kingdom that will save us.

The greatest evil, Jean Paul Sartre once wrote, is to treat as abstract that which is concrete. Yet critics of liberation theology often find fault with its theologians for this careful attention to a particular context, a particular community. Liberation theologians study the local context carefully because they want to see how the Christian message interacts with the environment. They believe that authentic faith arises out of the concrete struggles of human life, not from abstract principles. Yet critics of liberation theology reject this particularity, insisting that unity and uniformity of belief are essential for Christianity. The Roman Curia's reference to a "local church" is a diocese, or an entire province, not a particular grass roots community.

On their side, liberation theologians believe that to emphasize uniformity of church practice and human universality, often appealed to as the "brotherhood of man," is to hide and blur the truth about the daily lives of people throughout the world. They insist we must be presented with the "scandal of particularity" so as not to hide in the "escape hatch of universality." Anglican communities may experience similar tensions when they design worship services or strategies for outreach in accord with their particular racial, ethnic, sexual, or geographical context only to discover that they must "wait for the permission of theologians" (bishops or other officials) to determine if they may proceed at all. In the biblical account of Pentecost, after different races and tribes came together and received the Spirit, they returned to their own lands where they endeavored to live as local churches. Christian life since the earliest New Testament communities has been expressed in concrete places and communities throughout the world. For liberation theologians, unity lies in attentiveness to the Gospel and life in the Spirit. It is not the same as uniformity.

A second common feature of liberation theologies is their distinct theology of humanity. Like Anglicans, liberation theologians take human life as seriously as they take divine life; they do, however, emphasize a different starting point, the poor. Gustavo Guterriez writes that for the Gospel, the poor person is the neighbor par excellence. He adds, "It is not enough to say that love of God is inseparable from love of neighbor...love of God is unavoidably expressed through love of neighbor."

This preferential "option for the poor" has become one of the most controversial and misunderstood religious slogans since the Reformation spoke of "salvation by faith alone." It is not about God singling out the poor as the only recipients of the Gospel message, nor is it about choosing those to whom the Gospel must be preached. The Gospel is for rich and poor alike. Instead, a "preferential option for the poor" refers to the Bible's focus on the sin of oppression, which takes up the cause of the poor as opposed to that of the rich.

The poor, too, must take up their own cause, as this hymn to Jesus from the *Misa Popula* indicates:

> Because you are just
> And defend the poor,
> Because you love us
> And are truly our friend—
> We come today, all your people here,
> Firm and determined,
> To proclaim our worth and dignity.

Liberation theologians encourage all people to read the Bible and to look at theology from the viewpoint of the poor, taking their experiences and concerns as starting points.

Such a point of view is not a petition to do theology for the poor, nor is it a call for charity. The Roman Catholic Archbishop of Milwaukee, Rembert George Weakland, refers North Americans to the Pastoral Letter on Social Teachings and the U. S. Economy, which exhorts us all to see poverty in terms of justice and social structures, not merely charity and volunteer efforts: "Charity is always necessary but it does not get at root causes." The option for the poor holds serious implications for those of us who are not poor. As the South African theologian Albert Noland explains,

> taking an option for the poor is like setting out on a new spiritual journey. It is so easy to get stuck along the way, at the liberal stage of paternalism or at the romantic stage of glorying the poor. It is so easy to think that one has all the answers because of one's superior education or analysis. A thoroughgoing option for the poor includes the willingness to question one's assumptions and to learn from those who are oppressed. It is only after one has learnt to have confidence in the ability of the oppressed to promote their own cause and bring about their own liberation

that one can begin to share that struggle with them and to make a contribution in real solidarity.

Noland emphasizes the importance of our recognition that Jesus's option for the poor included encouraging them to take up their own cause, repeating that it was their faith that would heal them. Boff adds that other social classes may join the poor in this effort, supporting those trying to free themselves from oppression without trying to control the process.

For many people the problem raised by this option for the poor is not how to join in the struggle, but whether or not the Bible actually asks us to engage in the social and economic affairs of others. Many of us in First World nations have become accustomed to spiritualizing biblical messages, claiming that they have no reference to material realities. The Moffatt Bible Commentary advises, for instance, that Jesus's proclamation of Good News for the poor should be taken only in an inward and spiritual sense. For example, Jesus' reference to freeing the captives calls on us to liberate the *spiritually* bound, those enslaved to sin. The Bible does at times deal with spiritual captivity and deprivation, including the spiritual poverty of the Israelites after the exile. Yet liberation theologians believe that the Bible unequivocally challenges the glib ease with which we spiritualize and in other ways abstract Jesus's teachings. Robert McAfee Brown counsels us to hear the advice of the parable of the Good Samaritan (Lk.10:25-37), "Go and do likewise," as a clear command to mobilize ourselves, to move from "head trips to foot trips." The Bible is not a treatise in economics, but its overall perspective does view concentrated wealth in the midst of poverty, hunger and economic injustice as a sign of spiritual brokenness.

The spiritualization of the Gospel poses serious problems for liberation churches as well. Frei David talks of poor people giving in to a religion of easy demands and public religious occasions. He is not complimentary when he describes the Roman Catholic hierarchy's expectations for his people: "The Catholic poor should have babies, love Mary, hate Communists, mind their Pope, and leave salvation for the next world." Pablo Galdamez describes the "easy temptation" brought by North American evangelists who preach heavenly salvation in El Salvador:

> They closed their eyes to the scenario of sin and death being played out before them. And some of us succumbed to that easy temptation—the temptation to believe that you are serving God just by praying and reading the Bible and not getting involved in anyone's problems.

People throughout in the First and Third Worlds alike have to contend with this misuse of the Bible's teaching. Galdamez complains that "Jesus' message has been spiritualized and individualized to the point that its subversive force has been neutralized."

Asserting this "option for the poor," contending against those who would spiritualize the radical dimensions and demands of biblical prophecy, are behaviors familiar to Anglican leaders in this century from Temple and Case to Tutu and Heyward. Earlier in the nineteenth century F. D. Maurice led English church members in a movement that combined Anglo-Catholic liturgical revival, Evangelical preaching, and Christian Socialism. Maurice and J. M. Ludlow, an influential English social critic, were not interested in government ownership of production, but the new idea of producers' and workers' cooperatives. Both men labored for social reform based on Christian principles, and were equally committed to providing educational opportunities—including colleges for working men and women. Maurice and later William Temple would have agreed with Charles Gore that social justice was not "an adventitious addition to the gospel, but was its essential element." In 1924 an international, ecumenical Conference on Politics, Economy, and Citizenship (COPEC) convened under Temple's leadership. COPEC's assertions about the social relevance of the Gospel and the need for Christian scrutiny of economic and political life were similar to the agendas of today's liberation theologians. COPEC's participants would have concurred with Salvadoran Archbishop Romero's belief that "nearness to the world of the poor, as we see, [is] both an incarnation and a conversion."

A third emphasis in liberation theologies lies in their method of theological *praxis*. *Praxis* is a way of learning that encompasses both action and reflection. One of the best definition of *praxis* I know is Henri Nouwen's description of liberation theologians and churches as not thinking themselves into new ways of living, but living themselves into new ways of thinking. In *praxis*, theological reflection informs action for liberation; together there is an integration of thought (including theory) and social relationships. Jose Migues Bonino, an Argentinean Methodist, affirms that in liberation theology action and reflection are in partnership; the resulting activity is a mode of love. Latin American and other liberations theologians reject "abstract" theology. They insist we learn best by living fully in the present. I am reminded of lines from Thorton Wilder's play *Our Town*, Emily's plea from the windy hilltop graveyard of Grover's Corners:

> Emily: "Oh, earth, you're too wonderful for anybody to realize you . . . . Do any human beings ever realize life while they live it?—every, every minute?"
> Stage Manager: "No. The saints and poets, maybe—they do some."

The effectiveness of the *praxis* method is measured by the extent to which the quality of life is transformed by specific action strategies, which in their turn provide sustaining motivation for the ongoing liberation of the community. It is measured, for example, in progress toward establishing a housing cooperative, or in one woman's reflection upon the value of Bible study: "We did a lot of practical things . . . we talked about Jesus. We talked about the children." Liberation theologies seek to address directly the gap between proclamation and implementation. Pablo Galdamez reported:

> Gradually we discovered that the dichotomy between personal conversion and social transformation was a false one. After all, behind every personal conversion is, at least in seed, a social commitment.

Bonino concludes, "True worship and ethical commitment are one and the same. One is led to others in the same way that one is led to God." Simone Weil would have agreed: "The pursuit of God is never separate from the love of persons."

This *praxis* base of liberation theologies—steeped in consideration of the political, economic, and social as well as the theological realities of life—results in an ever more capacious doctrine of redemption. Liberation theologians speak of salvation as the fulfillment of three biblical promises: liberation from sin to communion with God, or what we might call personal salvation; liberation from cruel histories and debasing self-images, or cultural and theological affirmation; and liberation from oppressive socio-economic and political institutions, or civic and social freedoms. Gutierrez depicts Christ in the image of the Liberator who comes "to abolish injustice and build a new society." Liberation theologians write of salvation, repentance and the realization of Christ's reign on earth. Yet it is important to remember that for liberation churches and their theologians, salvation, indeed, all of theology, is not a set of ideas. Theology is instead the present-day work of God through graced, local communities. Why then are liberation theologies considered controversial among some Christians? Why is differentiation of belief from place to place, as long as it is deeply and faithfully rooted, a problem? Whose identity is challenged by the affirmations of liberation theologians? Why would some North American church members interested in promoting evangelization, ignore or dismiss liberation theologies?

Current criticism centers upon at least two charges. First, liberation theology has been accused of promoting Marxism, and its theologians throughout the world do employ what James Cone has described as a "common touch" of Marxism. They speak, for example, of class struggle; as we have seen, they also pay attention to oppressive dynamics between poor and rich. As Robert McAfee Brown notes, Marx may have coined the term "class struggle" but he did not invent the reality. At first it was thought that the current Pope, John Paul II, would condemn liberation theology because of its association with Marxist thought. Now it appears that even the Vatican does not dismiss Marxist analysis as a tool of the social and political sciences. Still, ideology is an effective means of separation. Others, including members of our own government, have used the label "communist" to distort perspectives from Latin American liberation theology. Marx is credited with calling religion "the opiate of the masses," yet in Latin America liberation theology is a stimulant to new life, not a drug that puts people to sleep. The presumed dependence on Marxism in local churches is, in practice, a sham.

There is, however, no escaping the second criticism—the fact that liberation theologies rigorously challenge many established institutions. The American Catholic theologian Robert Schreiter, in *Constructing Local Theologies*, distinguishes between liberation church models that promote social change and discontinuity, and institutional church

112

models that aim for uniform identity, continuity, and maintenance. The Vatican, a premier example of an institutional church model at work, silenced Leonardo Boff for eleven months in 1984-85. No doubt it was in response to his criticism of the clericalist nature of the Roman Catholic Church, and of others who act as if without clergy nothing decisive can happen. The subtitle (*Essays in Militant Ecclesiology*) from the most recent book published before his silencing has been replaced. There are those in the Vatican who perceive the popular churches of the *comunidades eclesiales de base* as a threat to the hierarchical church. When I was in Rome in 1979 as a member of an Episcopal-Roman Catholic dialogue, I distinctly recall being told by a leading Vatican official, Cardinal Hamer, that there were no such things as grass roots churches. Robert McAfee Brown recalls another cardinal's comment from Vatican II, "We don't need the guardianship of the Holy Spirit; we have the hierarchy." It is not surprising that the most creative and controversial work by Roman Catholic theologians today—whether by Kung or Schillebeeckx, Boff or Schreiter—is in the area of ecclesiology.

Recently the Roman Curia issued two position papers, or "instructions," on liberation theology. Apparently between 1984 and 1986 the Vatican moderated its response to liberation theology and decided not to attack its exponents in Latin America. Indeed the 1986 "Instruction on Christian Freedom and Liberation" concurs, using slightly different language, with the basic liberation theology emphasis that "it is therefore necessary to work simultaneously for the conversion of hearts and for the improvement of structures." The Roman Catholic hierarchy is beginning to come to terms with and learn from the local liberation theologies of Latin America.

North American Christians, however, have yet to acknowledge, let alone come to terms with, the challenges and insights from this vast new reformation in religion that is occurring south of our borders. Perhaps we too, like Vatican officials, tend to repudiate religious movements that challenge established religious, political and economic institutions. Perhaps we have succumbed to the "easy temptation" of a religion that "does not get involved" in social problems. If so, we are repudiating an Anglican legacy—one at least as old as the Protestant Reformation—that calls the church to strive for peace and justice in this world. From the perspective of the theological health of our own Communion, we have much to learn from liberation theologians.

Questions remain. How might Christians work for the improvement of structures? How will we respond to cultural changes brought about by evangelization of oppressed peoples? Must we choose between advocating liberation and maintaining our institutions? When members of one culture are changed through cross-cultural experiences, or when world-views seriously compete, how will we determine our wider loyalties? Are there important moral issues we have not begun to consider?

These are some of the questions raised by today's theologies of liberation that pertain to our future. Our spiritual welfare and ethical vision depend on our continuing response to liberation themes. As each of us who have been members of lively Christian communities know, the theology of a local church can impel movement forward in mission and outward toward others. The Christian message is, after all, about change, repentance, transformation, and salvation. The liberating God of Latin American and other liberation theologies, who loves us enough to disrupt our lives, travels with us as we journey onward.

IDEAS TO GROW ON

Making Room for the Future

It is not easy to think about the future. When I open my imagination to the future I receive so many messages that often I become overloaded, jammed, blocked. Messages seem to come at a faster pace than I can receive them. They overlap, making the messages I do receive unintelligible. Are my wires crossed? Are there too many people all trying to get through at once? Are we talking too fast? Is the speed of reporting news about change itself disarming? Is conflicting information causing at least minor distortion in all messages?

Admittedly, I have trouble finding time to think about the future. It is like my desk. There is more work calling for my attention right now in this busy present than I am able to process in any foreseeable future. I know persons, institutions, and even churches that are afraid to think much about their futures. There is a wonderful cartoon from the *New Yorker* magazine which, next to the Bible, is one of my favorite sources for interpreting contemporary wisdom. A nervous Charles Dickens sits across from a potential editor about to deliver judgment on the new manuscript before him: " I wish you would make up your mind, Mr. Dickens. Was it the best of times or was it the worst of times? It could scarcely have been both." We know the future is unclear, but what is the direction of its promise for the people of God? Should we be optimists or pessimists? Are there other alternatives?

We are told by the American social historian, Robert Bellah, that many of us have a deep uncertainty about the future, indeed that we have "a widespread feeling that life will be worse for our children." As a teenager in the 1950s I recall being told that most of us would not attain a standard of living equal to our parents'. To a degree this has proved true, but it certainly has not made my life worse or blocked my vision of the future. I sympathize with young people today who are tired of hearing about parents' fears for their lives, while preachers in local pulpits and on television frequently draw dreadful contrasts between a moral past and an amoral present. There is a long historical tradition of this kind of "future complaint" literature. It is aided and abetted not by accurate historical reconstruction, but by the distortion of nostalgia, the need to romanticize our pasts with sweeping descriptions of the "good old days."

Bad theology, as well as bad history, can, like nostalgia, lead to distorted messages and block our willingness to look to the future. The airwaves on Sunday morning are jammed with messages of despair: "doom and gloom" apocalyptic sermons or hate-filled panegyrics that describe how "others" are leading us astray. I used to think this kind of theology was not a part of so-called mainline denominations like my own. In this I was wrong, for I recently heard a mainline, North American Anglican theologian insist with apocalyptic certainty that this current generation was legitimately and fully "expendable." In *Sojourners* Tom Sine describes the threat caused by such despairing visions of the future:

> They not only threaten the cause of peace, but *they undermine the larger mission capability of the churches.* I am persuaded that the powers of darkness have pulled

off an amazing coup: while the American church un-
doubtedly is the wealthiest church in education, dis-
cretionary time, and money, a major segment of that
church has been lured, through its own bad theology,
to believe that it cannot make a difference for world
peace or social justice. As a consequence, many
Christians are taking their lives and resources out of
the mission of the church and not investing in the future. [emph. added]

Why are so many North Americans willing to accept despair
and disillusion about the future? Have we forgotten that the
biblical vision of the Apocalypse was given to instill refusal
to surrender to the powers of evil?

Liberation theologians are, as you may have noted,
refreshingly open to the future. Leonardo Boff, as if in
response to Mr. Dickens' editor, writes: "We are living *in
privileged times.* There is an upsurge of life in the church."
These Christians search for ways to change negatives into
positives. Black students in South Africa speak candidly of
"nothing to lose, a future to gain." The recently martyred
Archbishop of San Salvador, Oscar Romero, wrote, "It is
wrong to be sad. Christians cannot be pessimists. Christians
must always nourish in their hearts the fullness of joy. . . . I
have tried it many times and in the darkest moments, when
slander and persecution were at their worst." Boff concludes
his book on the people's church with the prophecy that the
Spirit of God will

revitalize the traditional and hierarchical institutions
of the Church. And, the history of salvation tells us
that where the Spirit is active, we can count on the
unexpected, the new that has not yet been seen!

Our contemporaries in Latin America are far from giving up
on the "mission capability of local churches." They are an-
ticipating new futures for their churches.

The contrast to most popular North American theology is startling. Surely we too live "in privileged times." We share a faith that invites all into a future where fear and hatred do not have the last word. We are as much in need of vision as our companions to the south. Yet when we take a long, hard look at our congregations, many of them seem to have little else on their minds but survival: not "Do we have a mission in this place?" or "Where can we go from here?" but "Will we be able to preserve ourselves?"

I have a colleague who works at a center for victims of domestic violence. She observes that it is not blood-letting but lack of imagination that perpetuates violence. Many batterers apparently believe that the only way they can be heard, the only way they can make others pay attention, is through violence. This form of communication is passed on in family systems from generation to generation. My colleague says that significant healing—physical, psychological, spiritual and historical—must enter into the lives of these families before they can imagine a different future. Looking backward and thinking forward is a part of the healing process.

In the Book of Common Prayer there is a prayer entitled "For Trust in God" and designated for use by "a sick person." When set in a collective voice, it offers families, institutions, churches, and other groups hope for the future:

> O God, the source of all health: So fill our hearts with faith in your love, that with calm expectancy we may make room for your power to possess us, and gracefully accept your healing; through Jesus Christ our Savior.

Healing points to the future. This prayer reminds me of the hymn text, "Let every heart prepare a home where such a mighty guest may come." Hospitality, making room for others, is essential. The Christian liturgical calendar regularly begins with Advent, a season of anticipation, expectation, and preparation for the new future heralded by Christ. Advent repeats the cycle of calling us to an uncertain but promising future. Whether our future days will be the best, the worst, or the most ambiguous, we are privileged to have an opportunity to prepare for, to make room for, the future.

When I prepare for future guests at home, I have to rearrange the basic furniture in my apartment and, since my study also serves as a guest room, I must even clear out the papers on my desk. In my experience this is best done not by trying to squeeze more into one room, but by clearing out what is outmoded or no longer essential for my current and future purposes. In our churches many of us have experienced less than successful future planning processes in which "work on the future" is loaded on top of already full agendas. Vestries and other church governing bodies are often caught up in the here and now. If we wish to envision the future, however, we must make room for this enterprise while trusting that even our most deeply held priorities might not need constant attention. We can ready ourselves by traveling lighter, abandoning unhelpful fixations, discarding old agendas. These and other preparations are conducive to reflecting on the future.

Letting go or suspending for the moment undue preoccupations with the present are necessary preludes to taking on—actually trying on—new behaviors. We can do this as we begin looking to the future. When I prepare to read a historical document, I consciously try to tune into the ways of hearing, seeing and judging used by those in past eras; I try to get inside their skin. Similarly, if we think perspectives on the future might influence our journeys, it is helpful to adapt our hearing, looking and knowing to the future tense. This does not mean that we will forget the present, for we carry what we know of the present, as well as what we recall of the past, into reflections on the future.

Theologically Christians already live toward the future. We dwell between the biblical vision of the promised reign of God and its realization in history. The American Roman Catholic bishops in their recent pastoral letter, "The Challenge of Peace: God's Promise and our Response," describe this time zone as "the already but not yet." This is not a resting place, but a time for asking, "What next?" Simone Weil has been described as one who lived the contradiction between the now and the not-yet. She worked tirelessly, relentlessly for secular justice as she thirsted for sacred truth. These seemingly paradoxical commitments may have sparked her most brilliant efforts. In what ways are we, like Weil, persons who live with seemingly contradictory but compelling commitments? In what ways are we, like many Latin Americans, charged with finding new ways of looking at our changing world, accountable to and capable of revitalizing life in our churches? As Carter Heyward and the other authors of *Revolutionary Forgiveness* ask, "To what extent are we responsible for our own liberation in history?" Will we invest in the future, in the mission capabilities of our churches?

Preparing for the future is not a new task for North Americans. In celebration of the Constitution of the United States, the *New Yorker* observed that the American experiment called for imaginative founders: "They turned for their power, their stature, to a source of power that seems flimsy to us today, but has instead proven to be sturdy: ideas." These leaders thought new thoughts and put their insights together with one another in service of the common good. Though these efforts were far from perfect and their ideas have been at best imperfectly realized, they launched an experiment in political life with the vision of a nation prefaced by "We the People" and with concrete ideas on which to grow.

The future continues to be a critical topic for North Americans. There is no mystery why. In addition to facing ethical challenges, some of which were described in the previous chapter, two of our basic social institutions, the work place and the family, are beginning to look different. The population of our streets and our shopping places changes as the ratio of young to old steadily diminishes, while the proportion of Blacks, Hispanics, Asians and other non-Anglo peoples in our population is increasing. Meanwhile, what of our churches? Are not congregations today living in a different world than that in which many of us were raised? How might we adapt traditional, timeworn tools to future commitments? What about our basic learning skills—are they up to the challenge of welcoming the future? What are healing, hospitable images that can both communicate and motivate new visions of the future?

What I have to offer in this final chapter are images and ideas to grow on. They are neither complete nor systematic. Nor are they are all brand new! These ideas and the questions they inevitably raise are meant for your acceptance, rejection, or modification, intended to invite and stretch our visions of the future. Perhaps in this cluster of impressions and convictions you will find suggestions that may be of service in the long haul.

As a historian I can offer encouragement to face the future. I am sure that we cannot "prepare" for the past, preserving for preserving's sake, trying to hold on to what is already lost. Our ancestors have lived with and through generation upon generation of changes. Many of our older citizens are skilled bearers of inspiration and innovation. As a theologian I can offer assurance that we are expected as Christians to transcend conventional limitations of time, to be at once biblically rooted and summoned into the future.

121

Renewing Perspectives

Sir Isaac Newton named his new reflecting lens for the invention we call the telescope, a "perspective." His designation is appealing because it more fully describes several advantages of this ingenious device. Newton noted that his "perspective" enabled him to see more clearly, which is the root meaning of this word; it also gave him a new way of seeing, a new perspective on the heavens. The telescope also magnifies. Because size and distance are often related, it gives the illusion of almost being there. As a self-confessed bird-watcher, I am enamored with Newton's gift and its usefulness in many fields: seeing more clearly, seeing in new ways, seeing as if we were "almost there." These are helpful proficiencies for Christians facing the future.

What is important to the work of discerning the future? The ways we look, listen, and ask questions. What we allow ourselves to notice, hear, and entertain. The practical tools we employ to focus, clarify, and interpret our discoveries. Most honest preachers know that merely talking about change does not create change without a shift in perspective. If we wish to do more than just "talk" about the future, we often have to adjust, improve, and change many of our basic learning skills—seeing, hearing, and inquiring. I recall two sayings from Civil Rights campaigns of the 1960s: "Go as fast as you can, as slow as you must, but go!" and "Change behaviors first, then minds."

The old adage "seeing is believing" offers a clue about where to start. Theologians today are using the term "paradigm shift" to describe life-changing shifts in perspective. "Paradigm" is a helpful word borrowed from the natural sciences, and it refers to the way a scientist sees the world and accordingly organizes and evaluates data. A paradigm constitutes the basic set of assumptions that define our world view. It is our primary perspective on life. A paradigm shift occurs when, over the course of time, even familiar data comes to take on new meanings until the scientist's or theologian's world is reorganized in a completely different light. When this happens there is a transformation in overall understanding, a conversion to an different way of seeing which eventually calls forth new methods and standards. In Newton's case his new perspective allowed him to see a bigger, brighter, clearer universe. On the basis of this change in behavior, he described and explained in *Principia Mathematica* how the universe worked. Paradigm shifts, in other words, indicate and occasion advances in human understanding.

Our Jewish and Christian ancestors endured and prospered through several paradigm shifts calling them to new futures, changes in perspective that allowed them to see anew. The birth, death and resurrection of Christ shifted the basic assumptions of our ancestors from the Old to the New Covenant. That was one shift. Then this revolutionary change in world view, which Paul called a "more excellent way", was soon followed by another, the conversion of the Gentiles. Both of these reversals, transformations in behavior and perspective, challenged early Christians to see more clearly, to see in new ways, and to continue looking toward the future. Paul wrote to the Corinthians, "For now we see in a mirror dimly, but then face to face . . ." (1 Cor. 13: 12). Reformation Christians experienced a paradigm shift through the introduction of vernacular bibles that allowed the laity to claim Scripture for their own. In our own time the "preferential option for the poor" in Latin America liberation theology is another reversal in understanding the nature and mission of the church, while feminist biblical and theological scholars are offering new knowledge and perspectives on women and religion. This process of reenvisioning reality allows us account for, not explain away, new information and achievements.

When congregations and other groups set out to explore the future, it is useful to know what to look for, to be prepared to notice the unanticipated, and to admit surprise. Many of us were raised in congregations of the 1950s. We lived in a society marked by rapidly expanding resources and in churches with burgeoning Christian education programs for children and youth. In the 1950s prevailing assumptions about successful congregations were related to growth, prosperity, expanding church schools and youth groups. These were the categories we were accustomed to notice and to value.

Today's churches face new realities, as Lyle Schaller, an authority on church renewal, advises us in his most recent book, *It's a Different World!* As the ratio of young to old steadily diminishes, churches would do well to take a long hard look at our aging populations. Now over 80% of Americans over 65 live alone. There are other changes we might notice. Since 1950, for example, women have become a new and growing majority of our population. The character, the face, of poverty is changing. Of the 35 million Americans whom the government defines as poor, most are women and children, with a disproportionate increase among racial and ethnic groups. Once theologians turned to philosophy as a tool to illumine theology. Now, in these latter days, the social sciences—economics, sociology, and political science—are useful tools in identifying what to look for, discovering a more accurate picture of the environment. The point is, we grow through truth rather than through fantasy. Although old stereotypes fade away slowly, it is necessary to move beyond the values and mission strategies of the 1950s. Then, we might have faced a decision between hiring a youth director or a director of Christian education. Today, we may face difficult choices about providing day care for children, supporting adult care for senior citizens who are in the early stages of Alzheimer's disease, or sponsoring a hospice for persons with AIDS.

What we choose to notice shapes our perspective on mission. Seeing more clearly involves different ways of looking at the world. It suggests a kind of bifocal vision that permits us to envision our immediate future and that of ourselves and others a few years hence. In his treatise on the Lord's Prayer Leonardo Boff describes another variety of bifocal vision. He speaks of the two "eyes" of prayerful theology: one always looking toward God, the other turned toward humankind. What we are not allowed is the luxury of peering from one eye only.

What we see and what we hear are often culturally conditioned. One of the ways I grow is by looking anew even at the most familiar setting; another is to listen more carefully even to the sounds in my own neighborhood. Sharpening our perspectives on the future may also involve tuning our listening skills. Someone once said of composing, "The song's already there—waiting to be drawn out of the air." The late feminist theologian Nelle Morton encouraged her students to "listen one another into speech." Referring to the Prologue of the Gospel of John, Nelle Morton insisted, "In the beginning [before the Word] was the hearing." Anthropologists studying new cultures tell of cultivating a "listening heart," hearing a culture before trying to speak in, or send messages to it. They expect, indeed want, the message to take on its own life in that local community.

Church officials who are not willing to listen and learn from voices in their own communities will be poor guides to the future. Listening today may be more complex than it was in the 1950s. Schaller writes that less homogeneity and greater diversity exist in today's congregations. I frequently attend a parish located on the edge of a metropolitan university. There are many different voices in this church: most members of the congregation are poor, a majority of parishioners are Black, a few members are university professors or students, and there are communicants (both Caucasian and Black) who are functionally illiterate. Listening is a critical, irreplaceable tool for members of this parish.

Listening our way into the future has to do with affirming, at the local and global levels, what we now call "pluralism." Although this term has been over-used and occasionally misinterpreted, pluralism remains a fundamental reality of our lives. It cannot be reduced to a problem, an enemy, or a gift, nor is it simply diversity, various cultural emphases, or divergent values. Pluralism is *different people*. The early Christian communities described in the epistles cultivated their assumptions about their new religion in a world where different people (including other Christians) held quite disparate views. In Corinth some were for Apollos, some for Cephas, and some for Paul (1 Cor. 1: 12). The process of building a community took time, struggle, and above all listening, inquiry, and reaffirmation.

Similar tasks face Anglicans today. At the recent Lambeth Conference bishops from 164 different countries gathered primarily for the difficult, concentrated work of listening and learning from one another. There are now over 70 million members of this worldwide Communion. Less than six million of us are from North America. The Episcopal Church in the United States has roughly the same number of members as the oldest Anglican Province in Africa—the Church of Southern Africa, whose current archbishop is Desmond Tutu. What might these two provinces learn from one another? Would not careful, reciprocal listening change at least a few of our most cherished assumptions? Given the many cultures within international Anglicanism, as well as the multitude of class, race, ethnic and other diversities among Christians worldwide, is there any other realistic way to face the future without embracing pluralism? I believe that pluriform knowledge of human experiences and cultures is more likely to enrich, rather than confuse, communication about values, and deepen religious commitment, too. With knowledge gained from listening and learning about our particularities, we may discover there are differences we need not overcome, as well as at least few truly universal values and agendas for the future.

Another way of facing the future and discerning new perspectives and directions is simply by asking questions. Questioning was and is an essential, enlivening aspect of Christian life. One of the earliest documents in the New Testament is Paul's letter to the young church in Thessalonica. Like others, this epistle is full of local questions. The Thessalonians were worried about whether those who were already dead would be united with Christ at the Second Coming (I Thess. 4: 13ff.)—this was one of their misgivings about the new faith. It was not Paul's most pressing concern, nor is it probably ours. Yet Paul prefaces his pastoral reply to their questions with these reassuring words, "We would not have you ignorant." Lack of understanding occasions active response, letter-writing, and dialogue if local churches are to continue their growth in the faith.

Christians today have their own local questions. As I travel throughout the church, I am asked tough questions about AIDS, abortion, and peace-making. Often these questions are posed by people who are afraid to raise them in parishes at home. If local parishes cease to be good places for asking contemporary questions and addressing critical cultural issues, the growth and maturity of their members will eventually be stunted. It is that simple. Inquiry is one of the ways we imagine the future.

It is a good idea to ask questions, even questions about the sermons we hear at home. Effective Christian witness, according to Dorothee Soelle, entails an ongoing process of indirect communication. In preaching, direct assertions are not enough. It is important to inquire, "What do you believe about what you have heard?" An older woman recently asked me, "Will my son be damned because he believes that Christians are not the best people on earth and good people belong to other religions?" She had worried for years about this question, not only because her son held beliefs that were not her own, but also because she had heard a sermon about evangelizing the Jews that led her to believe that her son would not be saved. She was afraid to ask her hometown rector about her son's open-mindedness.

In preaching, as well as on other occasions for learning, we can only gain from mutual inquiry. Newton's achievements were employed by other inquirers to gain new perspectives on more than one planet, indeed, more than one universe. Questions allow us to build on the experiences of others, to address our fears, to suggest new possibilities and imagine our way into the future. In this complex, fragmented world we owe it to one another to try on new perspectives—seeing, hearing, and asking questions in ways that may well advance our collective futures.

Seeking Hospitality

According to biblical scholars, the central and most scandalous practice of Jesus's ministry was hospitality. He not only offered bread and drink to strangers, spoke with tax collectors, healed women and other sinners, but also sat at table with outcasts, breaking fasts, Sabbath customs, and ancient taboos. Tampering with standard practice—picking grain for the hungry on the Sabbath, for example—repeatedly occasioned rebuke from religious elders and even caused murmuring among the disciples themselves. For these and other scandalous acts Jesus was accused of transgressing sacred tradition. Many sayings and parables reflect Jesus's radical ministry of extending and receiving hospitality. When the disciples of John complained that he did not observe the traditional fast and instead sat in the house with many tax collectors and sinners, Jesus responded,

> No one puts a piece of unshrunk cloth on an old garment, for the patch tears away from the garment, and a worse tear is made. Neither is new wine put into old wineskins; if it is, the skins burst, and the wine is spilled, and the skins are destroyed; but new wine is put into fresh wineskins, and so both are preserved. (Matt. 9: 16-17)

In order to usher in a new understanding of the God's reign, to imagine the hospitality of a society in which there were no outcasts, Jesus turned traditional expectations upside down. This ministry of hospitality was more radical than toleration of difference—Jesus challenged and reversed widely accepted religious conventions.

Throughout the centuries, however, we have domesticated, sentimentalized and spiritualized the radical, biblical mandate of hospitality. As with other biblical directives that command action in Christ's name, the obligation of extending hospitality to the stranger and the outcast still holds power to inform our mission. I suppose this is one reason why we teach our children the story of the Good Samaritan. Christians are a story-formed people. Our identity, exercise of authority, images of mission and understanding of tradition itself are illumined by this central biblical theme. What are new perspectives, new wineskins, for conveying hospitality today? In this concluding section I intend to keep one eye focused one the Gospel's call to hospitality and another on the shaping future strategies for Christians in mission.

Newfangled techniques and perspectives for envisioning the future, many of which I have just advocated, are not by themselves enough. Without our moorings, we may fall into greater passivity, complacency, or drift toward relativism. Guidance is essential for finding and improving our bearings as we move into the future. Tradition, for many Christians, provides these bearings. Yet I wonder, do we fully comprehend the implications of our claims on behalf of "tradition"? Members of one parish, for instance, will describe themselves as "traditional"; to them this means they are "normal"—they do nothing unusual or innovative. A sign outside another parish will proudly characterize itself as "traditionalist," and members of this congregation interpret their mission as continuing to use the 1928 Prayer Book and the King James Bible. Both of these parishes have limited, inadequate assessments of tradition's power. If our traditions are primarily about maintaining the status quo, or if we understand tradition as the expression of unmovable orthodoxy and turn it into an ideology, "traditionalism," then I believe we lose sight of the unexpected news conveyed in Scripture. In Matthew's gospel Jesus call this error "teaching as doctrine the precepts of men" (Matt. 15: 9b).

The historical theologian Margaret Miles has demonstrated that in word and in practice, tradition is naturally expansive. Social and religious conventions are always unfolding. Tradition is dynamic and growing; as such, it has a future. It is not to be hoarded like the treasure in the story from Matthew's gospel, which is buried in the ground and produces no profit (Matt. 25:18). When there are rapid social changes, or when a paradigm shift occurs, traditions often need to be addressed, reviewed, and where appropriate, reinterpreted. This can happen where we least expect to find change. One of my favorite illustrations is the replacement earlier this century of the militarist third verse of "God Save the Queen" from the first to the second version:

> O Lord our God, arise,
> Scatter our enemies,
> And make them fall;
> Confound their politics,
> Frustrate their knavish tricks;
> On thee our hopes we fix;
> God save us all!
>
> *to*
>
> Not on this land alone—
> But be God's mercies known
> From shore to shore
> Lord, make the nations see
> That men should brothers be,
> And form one family
> The wide world o'er.

Further alteration of this traditional hymn may yet occur.

By recalling and reclaiming biblical traditions, Christians maintain communication with the past and toward the future. Traditions are similar to artistic images—they have the capacity to reflect the intention of the original artist, and create compelling visions in the eyes of new beholders. Jesus found authority for his own teaching in Jewish tradition. When he read from the scroll in the synagogue at Nazareth, he both proclaimed and reclaimed the prophet Isaiah's command "to preach good news to the poor" (Lk. 4: 16-21).

Theology today is itself a reinterpretation of traditional theology. The fundamental biblical proclamation of good news for the poor was reinterpreted in the Tudor prayer books as the vision of a social commonwealth where citizens actively interceded for their neighbors, for "all sorts and conditions" of humanity. During the nineteenth century F. D. Maurice called Anglicans to address directly the ills of industrialization, while in North America Jane Addams established settlement houses to provide hospitality to immigrant populations decades before clergy spoke of social gospel theology. Today the option for the poor calls forth new actions among Latin American base communities, while in North America Episcopal churches designated as Jubilee Centers work and minister with poor people. The tradition of standing for hospitality to those who are marginalized continues to encourage new life and hope for the future. Whenever Christians make room for exploring their mission capabilities, it is good to inquire, "How do we understand and how will we communicate the central traditions of our faith?"

The identity of a local church, its concept of mission, may also determine whether or not it is able to move into the future. Our collective identity affects our ability to offer and receive hospitality. Early Christians concerned about extending the faith through missionary journeys discovered there were two dimensions to identity: the development of values that had to do with group boundaries, and the articulation of a world view that saw what needed to be explained to others. Identity is a gracious blend of knowing who we are in a given local setting, as well as knowing how we are related to others who are different. The dual nature of healthy identity formation is true for young people, new institutions and any person or group that experiences considerable change. When a congregation only addresses its internal identity, or when it outgrows a prior identity, its vitality and capacity for mission may be stunted. Congregations can become islands of provincialism, reservations cut off from their surroundings. Openness to others is as critical as loyalty to one's self. Mature Christian identity is always both local and multi-cultural. In shaping the future of local churches, it is helpful to begin by asking, "Who are we and how will we relate to persons who are different from us?"

I would not underestimate the strain of living with openness and integrity in a turbulent world any more than I would trivialize the identity crises which many young people experience, or minimize the difficulty of integrating the economic, religious and moral dimensions of our lives. Being challenged is part of being Christian. Richard Hooker believed that conflict was normal and only to be expected in growing churches. Therefore he paid considerable attention to defining several sources of religious authority. We have noticed how Jesus's ministry of hospitality occasioned conflict among religious authorities. It is now a legitimate cliché to say that Protestants have an "authority problem." This is an historical inheritance—with the use of vernacular bibles differences over the meaning of authority increased, as did the tension between maintaining uniformity and personalizing salvation. Given this legacy, it is not surprising that a recent North American consultation with the Archbishop of Canterbury addressed the theme of authority in crisis. Yet I think debates about the theoretical meaning and character of authority within Anglican and other Christian denominations can distract us from more central questions about the future.

I would prefer to ask, "What is to be done?" before searching for agreement on "Who is in charge?" Margaret Miles introduced me to the scholarship of Michel Foucault, a French philosopher whose recent work before his death focused on the need to act on the "main dangers" in our environment without first having to achieve agreement on universal rightness. "To act in this way," Miles continues, "with respect and gratitude for the actions of others, is to act *together* without needing to agree on principles, strategies, or immediate targets."

By practicing this kind of generous solidarity we might not be distracted by lesser problems, but rather get on with what Dorothy Sayers called "the work to be done." If a group or congregation agreed, for instance, that extending hospitality to poor and marginalized members of the local community was part of their primary identity as Christians, might not this vision inspire them to work through their traditional assumptions and internal differences? If the "main danger" was hunger, would not commitment to action build a more generous solidarity throughout the community? I am reminded of the missionary zeal of our American ancestors, of the woman who wrote, "I must be up and doing!" Scripture instructs us to be hearers and doers of the Word (Matt. 7: 24). Liberation theologians describe their faith as a "new way of living . . . not merely a new way of seeing and feeling." Tensions are a part of community life; they should not distract us from asking, "What is the central work we are given to do?"

Foucault's commitment to living into the future by focusing on the central work to be done is not only practical, it holds implications for building solidarity within diverse communities. He affirmed an ethic that measures strength in terms of relationships, as church members act together with generosity and respect. I am encouraged to accept this demanding challenge when I remember Verna Dozier's assertion, "God in Christ has already acted for us!" We can give up the supposition that we and our colleagues have to be perfect before we even start out. One theologian, Letty Russell, recommends "calculated inefficiency" in facing the future. I like this concept and think Foucault would have liked it as well, for it leaves room for growth and surprise, for imagination and learning along the way. Acting with respect and generosity toward others, including those with whom we differ, is recalled in the Presiding Bishop's insistence that there should be no "outcasts." Similarly the Roman Catholic bishops in their pastoral letters urge us all to "give up scapegoating," to stop blaming others for our own fears. It requires courage—literally "taking heart"—to face the "main dangers" in the environment, courage to set aside fears about diversity, courage to join in solidarity with others. In facing the future we need to ask, "For whom and with whom will we travel?" and "Who will go with us?"

Facing the future has to do with making choices. Our understanding of authority needs to be congruent with this freedom. William Temple wrote of human freedom, "God made men and women with hearts and wills that cannot be coerced but can respond freely, in order that there might be a fellowship of love answering the love with which [God] made them." In fact, a traditional view of authority is one in which people are obedient without losing their freedom. As most parishioners know, the exercise of authority varies among rectors, vestries, even among bishops. It is important to learn skills for working among different models of authority. The canons and polity of the church do not solve disagreements; there is room for choice and, often, many authorities are involved. The canons provide guidance for making decisions. Inevitably we must still inquire, "Who will be involved in making choices about the future?"

As we've noted, our biblical ancestors experienced competition among various religious authorities. In Pauline communities authority was incarnated in several different ways. There were charismatic leaders, synods and councils, people centered around households, and groups that Elisabeth Schussler Fiorenza has described as "communities of equals." Paul believed authority was dispersed throughout the people, all were bearers of the Spirit, all were

135

responsible for service. Leonardo Boff insists that early Christian authority was "congenial before it was monarchial." In order to move toward God's intended future, early Christians had to build congenial working relationships among persons with divergent experiences and expectations.

I was not always willing or able to agree with my twin brother, but as long as we were "congenial" we could talk and act together to accomplish desired ends. An ethic of responsibility prevailed, rather than agreement about which one of us was "right." I think many families have already developed skills in congenial authority. Side by side, often in the same family, denomination or church, we are becoming "differently abled" and more hospitable in making decisions. Congenial authority means a willingness to join in bringing a project, a task, a responsibility into being and perhaps to fruition. In developing choices about future goals and strategies, it is important to decide not "Who is right?" but "What values do we intend to affirm as we work together?"

Who are we, then, as we face the future? For centuries Christians have been inspired by the image of the Body of Christ, the most frequent of the New Testament's ninety-six metaphors for the church. Paul used this, his favorite metaphor for Christians, both to describe the future and to compel the hard work of seeking interdependence among Christians in the New Creation. This image of the church, of a whole ecclesiology, is also an expression of generous solidarity and hospitality. The Body of Christ in Corinth did not welcome strangers and competed even over their own spiritual gifts. Corinthian Christians were far from united. Paul's central requirement of this unruly people was not unity and certainly not uniformity; his central command was that the members of the Body of Christ "have the same care for one another" (1 Cor. 13: 25-26). This is a vision of sacrifice and suffering as well as solidarity.

Perhaps we have muted the radical, demanding character of this metaphor of the church and used it only as a facile injunction to unity. I believe our images, our North American metaphors for the church, must be renewed and strengthened so we may compel and motivate hospitality. Today Latin American theologians speak of the "Church of the Poor"; they remind us of an essential part of the tradition of hospitality—caring for the poor among the Body of Christ—that we may have forgotten or chosen to ignore. In our future thinking about ecclesiology Paul's metaphor should be more amply envisioned, joining the poor as the children of God with all other members of the Body.

These lines from a sermon given in Kenya by Joseph Donders reminds me that the Body of Christ is rooted in the concrete and specific.

> It is people
> who are the temple of God.
> All respect
> due to the temple
> is due to people
> to ourselves
> to each other:
> We are carriers of God
> in this world.
> And that is why
> it is very serious
> when we are knocked over our heads,
> or when we are knocking others
> over their heads:
> that is why it is very serious
> when people starve

or have to drink dirty water
or live in hopeless housing
or get blind
because nobody cares about the flies
in their eyes.
They,
we
are the temple of God.

When we speak of the Body of Christ as a metaphor for our own churches, we too should recall the biblically radical and publicly demanding character of this image.

In the recent past we also erred by envisioning baptism—the initiating, sacramental vehicle of hospitality—as a private affair. Alluding to Karl Barth's advice about concluding with a few words on baptism, we need to remember that baptism is the sacramental way Christians invite, receive and acknowledge hospitality. No one is initiated alone. No one is welcomed without friends or dispatched without those friends and guides whom we call "godparents." No one is sent forth without the expectation that they are welcome to return. Baptism is a celebratory group activity based upon movement that faces forward. This sacrament holds promises for the future—ongoing education in the faith, opportunity to learn and tell the story, and the invitation to join with others in mission. Theodore Eastman describes baptizing communities as moving us "into an unclear but promising future." Is this not what we expect for our children, our loved ones of any age?

We cannot promise a clearly defined future, but as Christians we can expect a promising one. The Body of Christ, the church of the poor, and baptizing communities are three living metaphors for a whole ecclesiology. They invite movement into the future. When we start out on a journey, it is well to ask, "What images of hospitality will inspire and challenge us along the way?"

A sense of direction is always helpful. As Pogo noted, "When you don't know where you are going, you're liable to end up somewhere else." A goal that is not shared is only a wish. It is not helpful to have private or superficial understandings of the people of God and our mission as a church.

We began by turning to the Bible for a sense of direction—seeking active verbs, encouraging words that summon us as God's created, chosen, sent, trusted and pursued people. In the testimonies of our biblical and other historical ancestors we found, in Thorton Wilder's phrase, "voices to guide us; and the memory of our mistakes to warn us." We heard again and again of their insistence upon renewal, education, and mission. We took a long, hard look at classical Anglican theology and recovered distinctive, hopeful characteristics for theology today. We reminded ourselves that theology is for the living. In Latin America we observed how a local community's liberation theology can empower and challenge us all.

Finally, we paused to consider ideas and images about the future. Laity as well as clergy, all the people of God, are essential in responding to sobering questions about the future.

The ethical struggle of moving forward in mission requires attentive inquiry and continuing engagement. Biblical, historical, theological, and contemporary resources provide courage for the journey. Hendrik Kraemer called the church "the community of the sent"; the world, he insisted, is the "church's working place." Despite tension, conflict and struggle, the good news is that Anglicans have usually been hopeful about this assignment.

In closing, I wish to join T. S. Eliot, with whom I began this journey of discovery, and bid my readers

Not fare well,
But fare forward, voyagers.

SELECTED FOR FURTHER READING

Chapter One

Brown, Robert McAfee. *Saying Yes and Saying No: On Rendering to God and Caesar* (Philadelphia: The Westminster Press, 1986).

_____ *Unexpected News: Reading the Bible with Third World Eyes* (Philadelphia: The Westminster Press, 1984).

Dozier, Verna. *The Authority of the Laity* (Washington, D.C.: The Alban Institute, 1982).

Guthrie, Jr., Harvey H. *Theology as Thanksgiving: From Israel's Psalms to the Church's Eucharist* (New York: The Seabury Press, 1981).

Johnson, James Weldon. *God's Trombones* (New York: The Viking Press, 1927).

Kraemer, Hendrik. *A Theology of the Laity* (Philadelphia: The Westminster Press, 1958).

Rowthorn, Anne. *The Liberation of the Laity* (Wilton, Ct.: Morehouse-Barlow, 1986).

Schillebeeckx, Edward. *The Church with a Human Face: A New and Expanded Theology of Ministry* (New York: Crossroad, 1985).

Stringfellow, William. *Count It All Joy* (Grand Rapids: Eerdmans, 1967).

Chapter Two

Addams, Jane. *Twenty Years at Hull-House* (New York: Macmillan, 1911).

All Are Called: Towards a Theology of the Laity (London: CIO Publishing, 1985).

Anderson, Owanah. *Jamestown Commitment: The Episcopal Church and the American Indian* (Cincinnati, Ohio: Forward Movement Publications, 1988).

Bonhoeffer, Dietrich. *Letters and Papers from Prison*, ed. by Eberhard Bethge (London: SCM Press, 1953).

Booty, John E. *The Church in History: An Anglican Interpretation* (New York: The Seabury Press, 1979).

Booty, John E., ed., Siegenthaler, David, and Wall, John N., Jr. *The Godly Kindgom of Tudor England: Great Books of the English Reformation* (Wilton, Ct.: Morehouse-Barlow, 1981).

Cooper, Anna Julia. *A Voice from the South* (1892; reprint, New York: Negro Universities Press, 1969).

Cranmer, Thomas. *The Works of Thomas Cranmer*, 2 vols. Edited by J.E. Cox for the Parker Society (Cambridge: Cambridge University Press, 1844-46).

Donovan, Mary Sudman. *A Different Call: Women's Ministries in the Episcopal Church, 1850-1920* (Wilton, Ct.: Morehouse-Barlow, 1986).

Douglas, Ann. *The Feminization of American Culture* (New York: Alfred A. Knopf, 1978).

Ruether, Rosemary Radford and Keller, Rosemary Skinner, eds. *Women and Religion in America*. Volume 1, *The Nineteenth Century: A Documentary History* (San Francisco: Harper & Row, 1981).

Sayers, Dorothy L. *The Mind of the Maker (London: Harcourt, Brace & Co., 1941).*

Underhill, Evelyn. *The Fruits of the Spirit* (London: A. R. Mowbray & Co., 1942).

Westerhoff, John H., III, and Edwards, O. C., Jr., eds. *A Faithful Church: Issues in the History of Catechesis* (Wilton, Ct.: Morehouse-Barlow, 1981).

Zikmund, Barbara Brown. *Discovering the Church* (Philadelphia: The Westminster Press, 1983).

Chapter Three

Believing in the Church, the Corporate Nature of Faith (London: SPCK, 1981). A Report by the Doctrine Commission of the Church of England.

Booty, John E. *What Makes Us Episcopalians?* (Wilton, Ct.: Morehouse-Barlow, 1982).

Erasmus, Desiderius. *Christian Humanism and The Reformation, Selected Writings,* a modern edition by John C. Olin (New York: Harper & Row, 1965).

Gibbs, Mark. *Christians with Secular Power* (Philadelphia: Fortress Press, 1981).

Hooker, Richard. *The Folger Library Edition of the Works of Richard Hooker.* Vols. 1 and 2, *Of the Laws of Ecclesiastical Polity, Books I-IV and V.* Edited by W. Speed Hill (Cambridge, Ma.: The Belknap Press of Harvard University Press, 1977).

Leech, Kenneth, "'The Real Archbishop': A Profile of Michael Ramsey," *The Christian Century* (March 12, 1986).

McAdoo, Henry R. *The Spirit of Anglicanism* (New York: Charles Scribner's Sons, 1965).

Micks, Marianne H. *Our Search for Identity: Humanity in the Image of God* (Philadelphia: Fortress Press, 1982).

Virginia Ramey Mollenkott, "To What End?" *Plumbline* (May, 1988).

Morton, Nelle. *The Journey is Home* (Boston: Beacon Press, 1985).

Soelle, Dorothee and Cloyes, Shirley A. *To Work and to Love: A Theology of Creation* (Philadelphia: Fortress Press, 1984).

Temple, William. *Nature, Man and God* (London: Macmillan and Co., 1934).

Theological Freedom and Social Responsibility (New York: The Seabury Press, 1967). The Report of the Advisory Committee of the Episcopal Church, Stephen F. Bayne, Jr., Chairman.

Wolf, William J. *No Cross, No Crown: A Study of the Atonement* (New York: Doubleday & Co., 1957).

Wolf, William J., ed. *The Spirit of Anglicanism: Hooker, Maurice, Temple* (Wilton, Ct.: Morehouse-Barlow, 1979).

Chapter Four

Boff, Leonardo. *Church: Charism and Power, Liberation Theology and the Institutional Church*, trans. by John W. Diercksmeier (New York: Crossroad, 1986).

Bonino, Jose Migues. *Toward a Christian Political Ethics* (Philadelphia: Fortress Press, 1983).

Brown, Robert McAfee. *Theology in a New Key: Responding to Liberation Themes* (Philadelphia: The Westminster Press, 1978).

Cardenal, Ernesto. *The Gospel in Solentiname*, 4 vols. (Maryknoll, N.Y.: Orbis Books, 1976-82).

Fox, Matthew. *A Spirituality Named Compassion* (Minneapolis: Winston Press, 1979).

Freire, Paolo, *Pedagogy of the Oppressed* (New York: The Seabury Press, 1972).

Galdamez, Pablo. *Faith of a People: The Story of a Christian Community in El Salvador, 1970-1980*, trans. by Robert R. Barr (Maryknoll, N.Y.: Orbis Books, 1986).

Gutierrez, Gustavo. *A Theology of Liberation: History, Politics and Salvation*, trans. by Sister Caridad Inda and John Eagleson (Maryknoll, N.Y.: Orbis Books, 1973).

Kramer, Jane, "Letter from the Elysian Fields," *New Yorker* (March 2, 1987, pp. 40-75).

Nelson-Pallmeyer, Jack. *The Politics of Compassion* (Maryknoll, N.Y.: Orbis Books, 1986).

Nolan, Albert, "The Option for the Poor in South Africa," in *Resistance and Hope, South African Essays in Honor of Beyers Naude*, ed. by C. Villa-Vicencio and J. W. de Gruchy, pp. 188-98 (Grand Rapids: Wm. B. Eerdmans, 1985).

Nolan, Albert. *God in South Africa: The Challenge of the Gospel* (Grand Rapids: William B. Eerdmans, 1988).

Oduyoye, Mercy Amba. *Hearing and Knowing: Theological Reflections on Christianity in Africa* (Maryknoll, N.Y.: Orbis Books, 1986).

Ricoeur, Paul. *The Symbolism of Evil* (Boston: Beacon Press, 1969).

Temple, William. *Christianity and the Social Order* (New York: Penguin Books, 1942).

Schreiter, Robert J. *Constructing Local Theologies* (Maryknoll, N.Y.: Orbis Books, 1985).

Wiesel, Elie. *Night* (New York: Avon, 1969).

Wilkes, James. *The Gift of Courage* (Toronto: Anglican Book Centre, 1979).

Chapter Five

The Amanecida Collective, Heyward, Carter and Gilson, Anne, et alia. *Revolutionary Forgiveness: Feminist Reflection on Nicaragua* (Maryknoll, N.Y.: Orbis Books, 1987).

Donders, Joseph G. *Jesus, The Stranger: Reflections on the Gospels* (Maryknoll, N.Y.: Orbis Books, 1978).

Eastman, A. Theodore. *The Baptizing Community: Christian Initiation and the Local Congregation* (New York: The Seabury Press, 1982).

Foucault, Michel. *The Foucault Reader*, ed. by Paul Rabinow (New York: Pantheon, 1984).

Koenig, John. *New Testament Hospitality: Partnership with Strangers as Promise and Mission* (Philadelphia: Fortress Press, 1985).

Miles, Margaret R., "Hermeneutics of Generosity and Suspicion: Pluralism and Theological Education," *Theological Education* (vol. 22, Supplement 1987, 34-52).

Russell, Letty M. *Household of Freedom: Authority in Feminist Theology* (Philadelphia: The Westminster Press, 1987).

Schaller, Lyle E. *It's a Different World! The Challenge for Today's Pastor* (Nashville: Abingdon Press, 1987).

Schussler Fiorenza, Elisabeth. *Bread Not Stone* (Boston: Beacon Press, 1984).

Thistlewaite, Susan B. *Metaphors for the Contemporary Church* (New York: Pilgrim Press, 1983).

Thompsett, Fredrica Harris. *Christian Feminist Perspectives on History, Bible, and Theology* (Cincinnati, OH: Forward Movement Publications, 1986).

INDEX

A

Addams, Jane 46, 52, 55, 132
adult education 13, 22, 24-25, 44, 50, 52, 54, 93
Anglican 32, 36, 38, 57, 59, 61-64, 66-86, 91, 94, 96, 101, 106, 109, 114, 116, 126, 132-133, 139
Anthony, Susan B. 47
authority 4, 14, 16, 35-37, 66, 69, 74, 85, 99-100, 124, 129, 131, 133, 135-136

B

baptism 15, 19, 38, 61, 63, 67-68, 96, 138
Barth, Karl 19, 138
Bayne, Stephen 67
Beecher, Catharine 43
Bellah, Robert 116
Bible 2, 4-8, 10, 12-14, 17, 19-26, 29, 31, 34-40, 44, 47, 57, 59, 61, 63, 65, 68-75, 80, 84, 102, 105-109, 111, 115, 123, 130, 133, 139
biblical interpretation 36, 74
Boff, Leonardo 102, 113, 117, 125, 136
Bonhoeffer, Dietrich 51, 56
Bonino, Jose Migues 110-111
Book of Common Prayer 8, 37-38, 67, 72, 78-79, 118
Booty, John 78, 85
Brown, Robert McAfee 7, 10, 25, 92, 102, 108, 112-113

C

Cardenal, Ernesto 104
Case, Adelaide Teague 53, 55
Catechism 8, 39, 67, 98, 105
church membership 41, 67
clergy 2-3, 5, 8-9, 21-22, 34, 38, 42, 47, 60, 65, 68, 71, 99-100, 113, 132, 139

Cooper, Anna Julia 42
Cranmer, Thomas 35, 38, 66, 69, 71, 77
creation 9, 13-14, 52, 63-64, 74-81, 85, 94, 97, 136

D

Donders, Joseph 137
Douglas, Ann 42
Douglas, Jane Demsey 30
Dozier, Verna 4, 6, 14, 69, 134

E

Eastman, Theodore 138
ecclesiology 2-7, 9, 17, 19, 113, 136-138
ecumenical movement 54
education for ministry 54
Eliot, T. S. 1, 4, 27, 51, 76, 88, 101, 140
Episcopal Church 8-9, 44-45, 48, 53, 62, 64, 73, 126, 132
Erasmus 68, 93
Eucharist 38, 63, 75, 78, 82-83, 96
evangelism 43, 61
Exodus 15, 89-90

F

Finney, Charles Grandison 44
Foucault, Michel 133-134
Freire, Paulo 103
fundamentalism 70

G

Galdamez, Pablo 104, 109, 111
Genesis 14, 61, 75
Gibbs, Mark 28
Gore, Charles 57, 82, 109
Grimke, Sarah 46
Gutierrez, Gustavo 29, 90, 103, 106, 111

H

Hale, Sarah Josepha 43
Hall, Joseph 76
Hartman, Sister Maria 102
Hebrew Scriptures 9, 14-15, 22, 38, 101
Heschel, Abraham Joshua 14, 101
Heuss, John 53
Heyward, Carter 95, 120
Holocaust 23, 50, 60, 97
Hooker, Richard 66, 70, 83, 133
hospitality 118, 128-129, 132-134, 136-139

I

identity 1-2, 5, 9, 11, 15-16, 22, 61-62, 64, 84, 88, 93-94, 96, 103, 112-113, 129, 132-134
Incarnation 20, 81-83, 85, 110

J

Jewel, John 66, 71
Julian of Norwich 96

K

Kraemer, Hendrik 3, 18, 54-55, 139

L

laity 2-5, 21, 28, 31-34, 36-39, 41, 49-50, 53-55, 60, 65, 68, 71, 99-100, 104, 123, 139
liberation theologies 89, 101, 103, 105, 110, 112-113, 123, 139
Luther, Martin 33, 36
Lux Mundi, 82

M

Maurice, F.D. 82, 86, 109, 132
McAdoo, Henry R. 85
memory 3, 27, 29, 139
Merton, Thomas 97
Micks, Marianne 81, 86, 96
Miles, Margaret 130, 133
missionary 18, 32, 41-43, 48-49, 132, 134
Mollenkott, Virginia Ramey 70, 79, 86
Moltmann, Jurgen 91
Morton, Nelle 125

N

New Testament 9, 16, 20, 32, 35, 38, 68, 81, 101, 106, 127, 136

Newton, Isaac 122-123, 128
Niebuhr, H. Richard 95
Noland, Albert 107-108

O

optimism 57, 66, 81, 85-86

P

paradigm 15, 122-123, 130
people of God 3-9, 13, 18, 21, 26, 31, 56, 62, 69, 72, 74, 80, 90-91, 95, 100, 116, 139
perspective 5-6, 11, 17, 22, 28, 31-32, 37, 40, 45, 50, 59, 77-78, 90, 94, 108, 112, 114, 119, 122-123, 125, 127-130
pluralism 49, 62, 126-127

R

Ramsey, Michael 82, 95
Ray, John 76
Reformation 8, 20-21, 29-30, 32-37, 39-40, 46-47, 50, 59, 63-66, 68-69, 77, 85, 89-92, 106, 113-114, 123
renewal 4, 32, 50, 64, 96, 102, 124, 139
Ricoeur, Paul 98
Romero, Oscar 110, 117
Rowthorn, Anne 31
Ruether, Rosemary 99, 101

S

Sayers, Dorothy 51-52, 134
Schaller, Lyle 124-125
Schillebeeckx, Edward 8, 103, 113

Schreiter, Robert 112-113
Schussler Fiorenza,
Elisabeth 135
Scott, Edward T. 78
Second World War 27-28,
32, 50-52, 56, 60, 84, 94
social reform 40, 45-47, 52,
55, 109
Soelle, Dorothee 79, 82, 128
Stowe, Harriett Beecher 43

T

Temple, William 51, 77, 84,
86, 94, 101, 109-110, 135
Tillich, Paul 98, 101
tradition 8, 23, 29-30, 37,
49, 54, 58-59, 62-63, 65-67,
75, 80, 84, 92-93, 116-117,
121, 129-132, 134-135, 137
Trilling, Lionel 98
Tutu, Desmond 86, 101,
109, 126

U

Underhill, Evelyn 51-52,
55, 76, 86

W

Weakland, Rembert
George 107
Weber, Max 77
Weil, Simone 51, 55, 111,
120
Wiesel, Elie 97, 101
Wilder, Thornton 110, 139
Wilkes, James 98
Wolf, William 83
World Council of Churches 54-55